Supervision of Literacy Programs

Supervision of Literacy Programs

Teachers as Grass-Roots Change Agents

Lawrence G. Erickson
Southern Illinois University–Carbondale

Allyn and Bacon
Boston • London • Toronto • Sydney • Tokyo • Singapore

Series Editor: Virginia Lanigan
Marketing Manager: Ellen Mann
Production Administrator: Marjorie Payne
Editorial Assistant: Nicole De Palma
Cover Administrator: Linda Knowles
Composition/Prepress Buyer: Linda Cox
Manufacturing Buyer: Louise Richardson
Editorial-Production Service: Chestnut Hill Enterprises, Inc.

Library of Congress Cataloging-in-Publication Data

Erickson, Lawrence G.
    Supervision of literacy programs : teachers as grass-roots change
agents / Lawrence G. Erickson.
      p.   cm.
    Includes bibliographical references and index.
    ISBN 0-205-16240-1
    1. Literacy programs--United States--Case studies. 2. Educational
change--United States. 3. Teacher participation in curriculum
planning--United States. I. Title.
LC151.E75 1995
374'.012--dc20
                                                 94-14444
                                                  CIP

Printed in the United States of America

10 9 8 7 6 5 4 3 2 1   99 98 97 96 95 94

To future writers and readers,
especially
Margaret and Jefferson

Contents

Preface

To All Readers

My primary intent throughout *Supervision of Literacy Programs: Teachers as Grass-Roots Change Agents* is to talk directly to classroom teachers about their roles as change agents, especially as it applies to improving the teaching of reading and writing. To do this, I cite reading and writing case studies and examples and describe how teachers act as grass-roots change agents to change literacy learning. My goal is to use the growing body of research, informed opinion, current practice, as well as case studies, to illustrate how teachers, acting as true change agents, are leading a "quiet revolution" to improve schools.

I have tried very hard to include only the change-agent strategies that are validated by research and informed practices. The case studies were carefully selected so that teachers would see that grass-roots, or teacher-led, change is not a mere dream. The careful combination of strategies and case studies in each chapter, as well as the narrative style of writing, is intended to bring clarity to what has traditionally been abstract and hidden.

The book has two parts. The first six chapters describe the processes, plans, and roles of teacher-change-agents. Chapters 1 and 2 define the change-agent role of teachers and lay the moral and professional foundation for this change-agent role. I also describe how teachers work outside the classroom, or "in the middle," to exercise their full professional role. Chapter 3 describes how change strategies must be selected to overcome the obstacles that always arise when the status quo is threatened. Chapters 4, 5, and 6 focus on specific processes that facilitate collaboration and implementation. My goal in this first part is to present a detailed description of *how* teacher-change-agents implement changes.

In the second part, the focus switches from "how to change" to "what to change." Chapters 7, 8, and 9 target three "what to change" aspects of the literacy context that go beyond the classroom and school. Specifically, I challenge you to work beyond the classroom to change the school curriculum, the community literacy base, and the literacy funding policies.

The goal of both sections is to present a detailed look at what working in the middle is like for teachers who, as change agents, operate as full-fledged professionals.

Finally, *Supervision of Literacy Programs* is a response to a concern I have encountered time and again for over 20 years. Most recently, this concern was interestingly raised during the same month in two different settings. One was within a group of school superintendents meeting in Southern Illinois; the other was at a conference of teachers and reading specialists in Milwaukee, Wisconsin. At the end of each presentation about improving school literacy programs, I asked these different audiences to write down their questions on slips of paper. I collected them and used them for a question-and-answer and discussion session. They asked:

Teachers' Questions

- How can we convince superintendents and school boards to support effective staff development?
- How do we go about changing the power structure for staff development? Right now the assistant superintendent decides.
- Do we start at the board level or the grass-roots level to get a cadre going?

Superintendents' Questions

- I want to know how to be more effective at assisting schools in making changes.
- I want to know how to help individuals work together to accept change.
- I want have a better understanding of the change process—to improve outcomes for students.

Notice that both groups have the same concern—implementing change. They accepted the worth of the ideas for improving school literacy programs. They agreed with the teaching ideas I shared with them, but they wanted to know how to introduce them into their schools and classrooms. This book is my response to a widespread concern about how to implement needed changes.

To Students

Supervision of Literacy Programs may have come into your hands because you are enrolled in a college class or workshop related to literacy learning and school improvement. You bring some prior teaching and school experiences to your reading of this book. One aspect of your prior thinking may be that you have considered, or even attempted, implementing changes that reflect your ideals about schools and students. Whether you were successful at implementing change, you will probably agree that improving the teaching of reading and writing is a most worthy and challenging task. This book is an attempt to clearly describe how teachers such as you act as change agents to make dreams about teaching reading and writing come true.

Although I cannot expect to convince each of you to be a change agent, I do expect that I might influence those of you who are truly concerned about your teaching and your students. I expect that, if your concern is strong enough, you will find some ideas, processes, and activities that you can use to make your visions a reality. In this regard, reading this book may change you.

True learning involves changing not only how we think but also how we act. Reading this book may change your thinking about what full-fledged professional teachers are like as we approach the next century. But taking some action to close the gap between what you are doing now and the vision you have for some future ideal is, from my perspective, the ultimate professional task. Of course, you, as a student, have a choice. For some of you, reading and thinking about change will satisfy your concerns. For others, the book may help you go beyond thinking about change. You will actually take some action to move you a bit closer to your ideals. If that happens you get my sincere praise. Sure, I wrote about change—but you did it!

To Teachers

My writing has been guided by several assumptions. These basic beliefs are based on current research and practice, as well as on ongoing personal experiences with teachers, principals, parents, administrators, and other professional educators. Specifically I contend that

- The basic issue in school improvement today is curriculum implementation, not curriculum development.
- Implementation is a function of the smallest unit—the single teacher and the single school.

- Teachers are the primary wielders of political power to effect changes in what happens to students.
- Teachers cannot wield this power alone. They must collaborate with other teachers and school officials to reach shared agreements.
- Teachers need new knowledge to become full-fledged professionals. This knowledge base is centered on adult learning, change agentry, and political processes.
- Teachers have the primary moral commitment to effect change. This commitment comes from their basic drives to have a positive effect on their students.

Writing about Change. As a college teacher or workshop leader with interest and expertise in improving school literacy programs, you are familiar with the literature on change agentry as it applies to schools. I suspect that you might agree with me that most of the respected books on changing schools have been written for consultants, specialists, and administrators, not for classroom teachers. This made sense historically because, until the 1990s, we tended to consider that teachers were the ones to be acted upon by change agents.

This book takes a different view. It was written from the perspective that the teachers are not the ones to be acted upon by change agents— rather, teachers are the change agents who act upon themselves and each other. The idea that the teachers are the change agents (which by itself is different) has caused me to use a narrative style of writing. I have tried to write as if I were talking directly to teachers, so I relied heavily on my personal experiences and metaphors. Knowing that these personal storytelling devices are limited, I illustrated major points with case studies of classroom teachers who were change agents. And finally, I resorted to more traditional book-type descriptions with step-by-step processes and many lists of sequenced events.

The result is a book that combines my personal experiences, current teacher examples, and current knowledge on school-based change agentry. I hope that the combination of these devices will work to help your students become better at implementing changes to improve literacy learning for students. As you use this book you will most certainly supplement it with your own stories, examples, and learning activities.

Settings for This Book. My hope is that, as you try to teach and influence others, you will find this book useful for several different settings. One is a graduate-level course that deals directly with improving school reading and writing programs. This book could be a primary source. The content and activities are designed to be used for class discussions, as well as class project assignments for individuals and small teams. I have used the manuscript this way and found that there is more than enough to do for a one-semester course.

Another possible setting is a graduate-level methods course in elementary reading and language arts or content literacy. In this type of course the methods book content would be the primary source of teaching ideas and strategies that teachers are to implement. This book would supplement this and show teachers how to implement these strategies, not only in their own classrooms but also with other teachers in the school.

This book will also serve as a guide in a workshop on change agentry. The participants could be teachers and principals from several schools, or from a single school. This book would be a manual for individuals and teams who want to implement changes in curriculum, instruction, or, possibly, school organization.

As a final thought on settings for this book, consider that, although the book features ideas on reading and writing, the change-agentry processes are applicable to other subject areas in the curriculum. The processes, procedures, and roles are applicable to a wide array of school improvement issues.

Using This Book. In addition to reading and discussing the book, the appendix describes ten activities that are designed to (1) review the material presented, and (2) practice and/or apply the concepts to either a real or contrived setting. I have used this material in classes and workshops and have had teachers modify them and use the processes and formats to make changes in their own schools. Here are my suggestions.

Use activities 1 and 2 with Chapters 1 and 2. Take plenty of time to reflect on and discuss both chapters. In addition, have teams of two or three work together to survey other teachers in their schools using activity 1. Activity 2 is a good way to preview the change-agent role of teachers. Use activities 3 and 4 with Chapters 3 and 4. These activities feature questionnaires and team planning items that small groups can work on in class together. They will get a sense of how to deal with conflicts, barriers, and team-planning processes.

Use activity 5 with Chapter 5. Teams of students work together to write a detailed improvement plan. They can use the eight-step process and the team memo in Chapter 5 to guide their writings.

Use activity 6 with Chapter 6. This can be done in a classroom, or teachers could try it out in their own schools.

Use activities 7, 8, 9, and 10 as small group or individual projects. These activities work well in a classroom setting, a workshop on school improvement, or in an actual school that wants to improve literacy learning.

Acknowledgments

Many people contributed to this work and they deserve to be acknowledged. On a personal level, my mother, Doris Erickson, died just as I was starting this project. Her special grace, energy, and intelligence continue to guide and inspire my life and work. Joan, my wife and best friend, read every chapter, and I am thankful for her editing, sense of humor, and absolute honesty.

Sections of this book were improved because informed reviewers took time to read and make comments. I would like to thank David Cooper, Ball State University; Vesta Mickel, College of Mount St. Mary; William Rupley, Texas A&M University; Karen Thomas, West Virginia University; and Wayne Otto, University of Wisconsin-Madison, for their insights and encouragement.

Thanks to Southern Illinois University at Carbondale for a semester of research and writing that enabled me to get a strong start on this book. The manuscript assistance from Karen Stotlar at SIU is truly appreciated, and the support of Virginia Lanigan of Allyn and Bacon has helped bring this project to completion.

Finally, I owe a debt of gratitude to many classroom teachers. Some of their stories are in this book. To all of the teachers who have amazed me with their energy, creativity, and commitment to being literacy leaders, I dedicate this text.

Supervision of Literacy Programs

Part I

Grass-Roots Change Agents

At the current time there is a major shift taking place regarding the role teachers have in school improvement efforts. Rather than passive audiences who are acted upon by change agents, teachers are becoming recognized as active and powerful change agents who, acting individually and collectively, change the teaching of reading and writing in school and community. The goal of section one is to describe how teachers carry out this role as true agents of change who implement improvements.

Chapter 1 defines the change-agent role of teachers, describes the moral source of the political power that teachers have, and provides historical background about how the recognition of this power has evolved. The idea of teachers working from the grass roots to meet with school officials "in the middle" is portrayed as the basis for teachers becoming full-fledged professionals.

Chapter 2 examines the unique "middle" role that teachers play in improving literacy learning in schools and classrooms. A case study reveals how teachers, as successful change agents, encounter and overcome a host of conflicts and barriers that threaten change.

Chapter 3 provides a broad, as well as detailed, look at change and conflict. The basic thesis is that, rather than trying to avoid conflict, it is better to select and use change activities to overcome the barriers that will surely arise. Because change and conflict go hand in hand, this chapter features a case study of how typical barriers are overcome by the long-range grass-roots efforts of teachers, the principal, and parents.

Chapter 4 describes how teachers, principals, parents, and others collaborate in teams to change reading and writing instruction on a schoolwide basis. Because teachers tend to work alone, collaboration is in itself a major change. The case study example in this chapter illustrates how shared agreements and a collective "voice" lead to implementing change.

Chapter 5 is a step-by-step description of how teams "dance" together to implement changes in reading and writing instruction. These steps are crucial to successful attempts at working in the "middle." These steps represent new knowledge and skills that teachers use as they exercise their full professional role.

Chapter 6 describes a variety of adult learning activities that teachers use to implement changes. The 17 learning formats presented in this chapter are carefully selected on the basis of their usefulness, practicality, and success. Altogether the content in these first six chapters is intended to be one package of information basic to the "how" of change agentry for teachers.

Teachers As Literacy Leaders

*We know what we will have if we operate as we have
in the past—and the prospects are not promising.**

We were eating scrambled eggs on the wicker-furnished porch of an overdecorated bed-and-breakfast in Northport, Michigan, in August 1990 when the conversation at our table moved from sharing names and hometowns to what we do. The other vacationing couple, from Detroit, kept a sailboat in the Northport harbor and the husband owned an auto-industry-related business. When he heard that I was a professor who taught teachers, he asked something like, "Who do you think should be in charge of school reform? The federal government, the state governors, or how about businesses?" I said, "Teachers! Teachers are often thought to be the problem when they really are the solution." He didn't jump in, so I started to say more, when my wife gave me her half smile that means "Cool it." However, I was committed and continued, "In my work I have found that many experienced teachers and principals have a vision of what school should be for them and their students." I said, "The trick is not so much to reform as it is to renorm our thinking about school improvement, and allow teachers and principals to work toward making

*Carl D. Glickman, 1992. *Supervision in Transition,* p. 1.

their visions a reality." With that sort of breakfast minilecture off my chest, I sipped my coffee and took a second muffin.

As I recall, my wife then tactfully turned the conversation toward the day's vacation activities, and I was able to stop lecturing. I thought to myself, "Don't ever ask a professor a question if you don't want a lecture." And I have thought about this vacation scene in another sense, too. Was my response valid? I hadn't really planned to talk about school issues at breakfast. Do I really believe teachers should be in control of school improvement or was I just showing off by giving an unexpected answer to a sincere question? To be perfectly honest, I think it was a little bit of both. I know I enjoy giving unexpected answers. I think I can get a laugh that way, and perhaps I have a competitive need to startle others. On the other hand, I truly believe that teachers are the solution, not the problem, in schools. I also believe no one sector of society can be in charge of school reform. The responsibility for that is shared by parents, teachers, school officials, and, of course, the political leaders who represent the citizens.

Why then did I tell my fellow bed-and-breakfasters that teachers should be in charge? My guess is that at this time in my work I have had enough experiences to unlearn some old ideas. Only in the last five years have I fully appreciated the true potential that teachers have for leading bottom-up change. This has not always been the case.

In my first "life" in the 1960s I split a dozen years between an elementary classroom and an elementary principal's office. Then, after a Ph.D. and a brief year as a central office reading consultant, my second "life" as a reading professor started in the early 1970s.

During the first dozen years of this second life I operated for the most part as a top-down change agent. That is, I assumed that schools would change if I could influence the political and educational leaders to get the right laws and policies adopted. So I worked with state-level curriculum and assessment programs and developed materials and led "Right to Read" workshops for curriculum specialists, principals, and teachers. And I wrote and practiced about how to do more effective in-service education to improve the teaching of reading. All the while I viewed change from the top-down perspective that the change agents were those with status who, because of their position and expertise, were expected to act upon others and lead them from the front. The "others" of course, were teachers, and I, of course, was the change agent. I think Calvin illustrates this very nicely in this cartoon. Exactly when I realized that this was probably a false assumption is hard to pinpoint. I'd like to say I made a brilliant rational decision to try to influence others with a different approach. But that would be untrue. Like most insights I realized this one after it had already occurred.

Renewal Leads to Change

What happened goes like this: It was 1986 when excited and motivated teachers were raving about changes they had made, or were making, in their teaching. The teachers were participating in workshop classes I was team teaching with faculty from the English department. The workshops were part of a public school/university arrangement that started in 1985 at Southern Illinois University in Carbondale. The idea behind the Renewal Institute for Practicing Educators (RIPE) was to get experienced teachers back to college with tuition-free classes as an incentive. When they did return, they would have classes taught by faculty from both education and the liberal arts and sciences. I talk more about RIPE later in the book, if you want more details. For now, let's just focus on the fact that RIPE participants were going back to their classrooms, making changes, and influencing other teachers about better ways to teach reading and writing. Now in 1993, after seven years of watching what RIPE teachers are doing back in their classrooms, I find several reasons to justify my belief that teachers are change agents.

An important point is that RIPE participants were mainly experienced, mid-life teachers who volunteered to come. For the most part, they had a minimum of ten years' experience, they were active in their communities, they were married, and their children were teenagers or older. They had many concerns about schools and some of them were almost burned out and were looking for work outside of schools. They were questioning their worth and they were seeking ideas that they could

Calvin and Hobbes  by Bill Watterson

FIGURE 1-1

implement. And apparently RIPE helped. They were reading about how language is learned and what happens when reading and writing are taught together. They visited classrooms and listened to panels of teachers who were implementing holistic and meaning-based literacy lessons. RIPE classes had few lectures and no tests. Instead, participants read many current articles, sat in a circle, and talked and talked with instructors and each other. We expected them to implement a teaching idea in their classroom and report back to everyone else. And to help them implement changes we had a large collection of teaching materials (videos, software, children's literature, etc.) that they could take to use with their students. In addition to a large collection of books, videos, and software that they could use to pursue their own learning, we had them visit each other's classrooms and we drove all over the area visiting their classrooms. These follow-up visits confirmed that changes were taking place. What was happening? What was different? RIPE had initiated something and the changes continue. And I think I can tell why.

When experienced teachers voluntarily study common articles, share concerns, take some action, and are supported by fellow teachers, professors, and materials, a critical mass—a community of learners—is created. This critical mass created new energy that empowered teachers to take some action. Remember, they were, for the most part, veteran volunteers who were seeking changes in their teaching. And when they came looking they were given choices. We selected the articles and started discussions at early meetings, but there were no tests or papers to write to satisfy typical higher education demands. Instead, as one teacher said, "you tended to lead from behind." The workshop was a forum that downplayed our academic power in favor of letting the veteran teachers act upon their concerns.

Teacher Voices and Visions

During RIPE's interactive workshop, with its focus on language learning, we did not only talk about how we help students find their "voice." The intense discussions and the articles on children's writing led the teachers to hear their own and other teachers' voices. And what they heard is what Fullan (1993) calls their clear sense of moral purpose "to make a difference in the lives of students" (p. 12). Many of these veteran teachers expressed the idea that they were at a point in their careers in which they experienced various shades of burnout. They had begun their careers with a clear sense of moral purpose about making a difference. This had been dissipated over time by what Farber (1991) calls a gradual sense of "inconsequentiality." But during the workshop, the teachers encountered voices that helped them hear the moral voices that led them to teaching in the first place. The voices came from articles, from each other, from a panel of enthusiastic teachers, from watching other teachers, and from seeing what children produce as they become increasingly more literate. As the teachers regained this moral vision, the workshop took on a new flavor.

I could mark the points at which the teachers' voices took control over the professors' voices when they began to use their "J" and "B" cards. Let me explain. The professorial urge to lecture or lead from the front is very strong, but the teachers devised a good mechanism to control this. Whenever we start to take over and theorize too much, the teachers will hold up *J*, or jargon cards, to remind us to stop talking. They also created *B*, or break cards, to remind us that they had been sitting too long and needed to take a walk to the rest room or get something to drink.

A Return to Moral Purpose Led to Change

Propelled by their moral voices and visions about making a difference in their student's lives, the teachers readily took chances, risked some failures, tried new techniques, shared successes and failures with others, and were acting rejuvenated and excited. In short, they didn't need anyone to lead them. It was more like being on the sidelines watching, cheering, and maybe coaching when our advice was asked for. And even when they went back to their schools they didn't need a principal to lead them. We interviewed and surveyed a sample of RIPE participants and found that principals were neutral regarding change (Erickson, 1991). Principals didn't help and didn't hurt. For the most part, experienced teachers and principals seemed to respect each other's territory and keep out of each other's way.

In addition to the RIPE experience, the literature on teachers as the change agents supports my own grass-roots orientation. I believe Fullan (1993) is exactly right when he writes that "teachers must combine the mantle of moral purpose with the skills of change agentry" (p. 12). He goes on to write:

> *On the one hand, schools are expected to engage in continuous renewal, and change expectations are constantly swirling around them. On the other hand, the way teachers are trained, the way educational hierarchy operates, and the way political decision makers treat educators results in a system that is more likely to retain the status quo. One way out of this quandary is to make explicit the goals and skills of change*

agentry. To break the impasse we need a new conception of teacher professionalism that integrates moral purpose and change agentry, one that works simultaneously on individual and institutional development. One cannot wait for the other (p. 12).

This book is about how teachers are breaking the impasse as they individually teach students and collectively change the status quo.

Many recent books and articles on adult learning, staff development, and educational change support the thesis of teachers as change agents. I will be citing research frequently throughout the book that points to the effectiveness of bottom-up change. These findings, along with my current and direct work with teachers, lead me to believe that teachers (and to a somewhat lesser extent, principals) are not mere conduits of knowledge—they are the knowledge. Effective teachers cannot be separated from facts, ideas, concepts, processes, or whatever they teach. There is a holistic quality to teaching and learning that says teachers are not merely conduits that society can train and pour information through and into students. I think it is a fallacy to view a teacher as just a conduit, container, or pipe that transports or delivers ideas and/or concepts to students. A truly effective teacher is one complete package of both content and processes. This simply means that we cannot think of change agents as being separate from teachers. We need to visualize the teacher and the change agent as one complete package.

Teachers Have the Power

The significance of classroom teachers is not a new idea. The most important reading research in the 1960s and 1970s concluded that the teacher, not the method or materials, is ". . . the single most important variable within the learning environment . . ." (Vacca and Vacca, 1979; quoted in Pearson, 1992). In light of this conclusion, it is noteworthy that the most prestigious school-reform proposals in the 1980s treat the teachers as the "problem" that must be fixed. The "fixers" are, of course, "experts" from the central office, the universities, and businesses. In one analysis of several major reform proposals, the reviewers (Stedman and Smith, 1983; cited in Dougherty and Hammack, 1990) indicated that in reference to teachers, the recommendations are "Silent on pedagogy, [and] the reports suggest only one way to improve the quality of teaching, and that is to improve the quality of teachers" (p. 662). The assumption that low-quality teachers are the problem has led to a flurry of mandates from above and outside the classroom. And we now know from studies of school effectiveness that improvement is a function of the commitment of the teachers, not top-down mandates (Stedman and Smith, p. 664). In this book I am going farther than the vague idea of teacher commitment. I am extending commitment and asserting that many experienced teachers are the change agents. They are already committed to a vision of how to make literacy learning better for their students, and they are already at work. And some of them will be featured in later chapters.

Therefore, while this book is intended for experienced classroom teachers and other educators who desire to improve reading and writing instruction, it has another important purpose. The case studies and comments describe how experienced professional teachers are exercising their potential as grass-roots change agents. For teachers who are already taking the lead, this information is but testimony to their effort and success. However, for some others, the stories and accompanying notes are intended to provide information that may enable them to make their visions of classrooms and schools a reality.

The Evolution of Teachers As Change Agents

Traditionally, most educators, including teachers themselves, have not considered classroom teachers to be change agents for school reform. Instead, teachers are viewed as subordinates in a hierarchy that features control from the top down. In the 1960s and continuing through the 1970s, unionism "... partially helped teachers obtain an authoritative voice . . ." (Pearson and Hall, 1993, p. 172). In the early 1980s, reform movements proposed to attract talented and creative individuals to teaching with career ladders, merit pay, and college-loan incentives. But many talented students shunned teaching as a career because they perceived the frustrating working conditions and lack of control that teachers experience (Berry, 1986). Later 1980s and current reforms propose that teachers will have to be more autonomous and creative in order to produce students who can think critically, create, and keep learning on their own throughout life. Current reform rhetoric of the 1990s, such as site-based management, collaboration, and team decision making, require that teachers have more autonomy.

But the gap between the rhetoric and reality of teacher autonomy remains. For a long time, schools have been structured and operated so that principals, curriculum specialists, administrators, policy makers, and professors viewed the teacher as someone whom change agents acted upon. This bureaucratic model holds that teachers are workers who must be supervised, managed, evaluated, and changed by an expert from above or from outside. Teachers have learned to accept this as a way of life, and many tend to keep quiet, stay behind a closed classroom door, and make changes quietly and alone. For many teachers and principals the bureaucratic model is still the norm.

For example, McClure (1988) describes how his initial efforts to get teachers and principals to collaborate to improve schools was impeded by the following closed-door beliefs and practices:

1. Principals and teachers relied heavily on manuals, mandates, and directives from above, and advice from outside the school.
2. School staffs tended to be conservative. They felt past change efforts had done more harm than good. They felt it was their responsibility to prevent change and protect the school.
3. Principals and teachers did not view themselves as risk takers. They viewed schools as organizations uninterested in input from those at the lowest levels. Schools punished those who took risks.
4. Principals and teachers accepted control from outside and above. They accepted standardized tests, textbook manuals, behavioral objectives, and other controlling technologies.

These views represent years of belief and practice that affirmed a "labor and management" notion that teachers have, at best, a passive role in the content and process of changing schools. Given this view of the teacher, it is no surprise that many school improvement efforts into the 1990s still reflect a top-down approach to change.

However, although many of the school improvement initiatives of the 1980s pushed new teacher education requirements, certification testing, and new evaluation policies, they also reflected modern management ideas that departed from the old bureaucratic model. During the 1980s over 1,000 acts of legislation were aimed at "professionalizing" teaching (Darling-Hammond and Berry, 1988). Many of the reform proposals of the 1980s were based on the assumption that teachers must play an active role in crafting improved techniques and methods. This professional orientation acknowledges that, in the face of the diverse needs of students, teachers make ongoing and complex decisions in order to effect learning. The reform proposals that acknowledged the active and fluid nature of learning and teaching spawned a new view of the teachers' role in changing schools. Instead of being inspected individually by an expert with a checklist, we began to see in the 1980s teachers examining their own and each other's work, deciding what works, looking at alternatives, and helping each other change. This active role by teachers in school reform has evolved to the point where now, in the 1990s, an increasing amount of evidence reveals that, despite the history of being the lowest on the totem pole, teachers are beginning to take their rightful place as powerful and professional change agents. Grass-roots change agentry is emerging as another reform strategy.

Since the mid-1980s a rapidly increasing number of books, articles, and reports from across the nation acknowledge how empowered teachers are the agents of change in school literacy programs. Studies of school policies revealed that teachers had tremendous political power to control what happened behind their closed classroom doors (Meek, 1988). Policy analysis experts and researchers such as Linda Darling-Hammond (1988) and Bracey (1991) looked at years of top-down mandates and reported that teachers must be listened to and that improved teaching practices cannot be mandated.

Fraatz (1987) studied reading classes and found that the single teacher has perhaps too much power over literacy learning. She recommended that shared decision making through collaboration and negotiation is imperative to making changes. Throughout the 1980s the notion of collaboration caught on and schools began to make new arrangements to listen to teachers. Today in the 1990s we have moved ahead a bit, and more and more reports of site-based management and other collaborative efforts have paved the way for the current thesis: that the teachers are the important change agents. Like any evolution, the process of altering a strictly top-down view of change to include a strong bottom-up effort is slow in coming. It will be resisted by educators in general and teachers in particular. This book describes how some teachers and schools are dealing with the shift from mandates from above to collaboration from within. Case studies and models are presented to illustrate how teachers are learning to work with each other as change agents for improving literacy learning.

Working in the Middle

Although teachers have the most control over what happens to students on a daily or immediate basis, long-range improvements in literacy learning will need more than teacher efforts. Lasting improvements require the shared responsibility and power that comes when everyone in the school and local community works together. What this means is that teacher-directed bottom-up or grass-roots change arrangements still need some political protection from the top (Fiske, 1991). Full-blown improvements in school literacy programs happen when teachers start in the classroom and work "up," while others at the top or district and system level work "down" to protect and support classroom changes. The goal is to meet somewhere in the middle like tunnel builders. This book is an attempt to describe what this middle is like for teachers and principals. The case studies, the change procedures, reading-improvement teams, the change formats—all describe what is happening in the middle of the tunneling process. Just how do those at either end of the tunnel successfully meet in the middle? They negotiate plans that accommodate both top-down and bottom-up concerns.

This type of teamwork reveals a significant values shift. School leaders who used to rule by administrative directive are learning to delegate and accept shared responsibility for student learning. Teachers who are used to following directives and shunting responsibility to others are trusting themselves and accepting responsibility for change. These new roles represent a significant values shift that requires new information for both teachers and school leaders. Notice, in the following case study, how Kelly had to work in the middle to implement change.

Working Alone

In my first year of teaching I was hired to teach fifth grade. At the same time three other new teachers were also hired to teach fifth grade at other schools in the district. I was assigned to a small school with one fifth grade, so I began my teaching separated from the other three.

All four of us had attended the same teacher education program and we were interested in teaching reading using a literature-based approach rather than a basal reader. At the beginning of the school year I approached my principal on my own with my plan to use children's literature rather than the basal reader.

He was very supportive and encouraged me but, because he was also newly hired, he referred me to the district reading coordinator. The coordinator told me that because I was a new teacher I would be required to teach from the basal series. She also pointed out that the teacher I replaced had already ordered all of the reproducible and consumable materials that accompanied the basal, so there was no money to buy paperback books. She did say I could supplement the regular series with novels if I could provide them out of my own pocket.

The principal suggested that we contact businesses for money to buy novels. He was very supportive and called several businesses. But he found that my three colleagues at the other, larger school had already enlisted the help of their parent organization. The businesses my principal contacted told him that they had already donated to provide the five fifth grades at the larger school with sets of novels.

The principal did not approach our parent group. He was new, the parents in our school were not very active, and the parent group had had problems during the previous year and was being restructured. So during my first year I did not implement a literature-based reading program.

Yet I did not give up on my dream. After one year of using the basal, the workbooks, the ditto sheets, and the tests, I was even more firmly convinced of the benefits of using interesting literature and novels to teach reading. I also had gone back to school and enrolled in graduate classes, where I made contact with other teachers who were struggling to implement changes in their school. I gained enthusiasm and expertise as I heard how they were implementing literature-based reading in their rooms.

Working in the Middle

When I went back to teach fifth grade for my second year, I renewed my effort to have the district buy novels for my classroom. But this time I had learned that the curriculum director and the reading coordinator had met with teachers at the larger school. Teachers from other schools were not invited. I found out that the teachers at the larger school had asked for and received money to buy novels for the fifth-grade classes. After confirming this with the reading coordinator, she suggested that I meet with the curriculum director.

When I met with him I suggested that because he was willing to buy novels for the other school he should also fund our school. I suggested that instead of ordering any consumable materials that accompanied the basal series we should use the money to buy sets of novels for my classroom. He agreed but insisted I find the lowest prices. He said that my reading program must meet the district and state reading goals. I assured him I knew how to do this and I would meet this objective.

I then went to the president of the newly formed parent organization at our school. Her daughter was in my class, so it was easy to talk to her. I told her how the district would fund the purchase of novels and I asked her if the parent group could match those funds. She was very supportive and asked me to make a presentation at the next parent meeting, at which she would ask for a motion to vote on the purchase of novels.

As I prepared my presentation I enlisted the help of other teachers in my building. They were supportive and agreed to be at the meeting to vote "yes." For my presentation I selected two novels, *Where the Red Fern Grows* and *The Borrowers*. Parents at my school are conservative, and I did not want to cause controversy about language or content. At the meeting I reviewed the state and district reading goals, I talked about the state and district testing, and I explained that in order to do well on these tests students need to read different types of good literature. I told them how reading good novels would help students enjoy reading and lead them to be independent and life-long readers. The parents voted to spend money on the novels, and so with the district and parent funds, I had four novel sets to build a literature-based reading program.

Continuing to Work in the Middle

After two years I have expanded my novel sets and I continue to provide meaningful reading and writing experiences based on literature. My program changes somewhat each year to meet different needs and interests. I enjoy this approach and feel revitalized as a teacher when I see students improve and become excited about what they read and write. The students' enthusiasm and love for a literature approach is the biggest motivator for me.

I understand why teachers are often reluctant to implement changes. It takes a lot of time and effort to do the research and preparation. But teachers can initiate changes. My efforts seem to be paying off. Along with my classroom success I was asked by the reading coordinator and curriculum director to work on a districtwide committee. Our task is to research newly published literature-based programs that might be implemented districtwide. These administrators are now aware of the positive effects this approach is having with students, parents, and teachers (Atkisson, 1992).

While this book presents more of the teacher's side of this values shift, the information is important to those who work outside the classroom. As many wise school leaders know, no single person or element of the "system," no matter how loud or powerful, can force improvements on others. Principals, supervisors, curriculum coordinators, superintendents, and board of education members need to consider teachers as the primary change agents, especially for improving school literacy learning. Likewise, teachers need to know why and how to gain the support of the administration and the community. They need to know the skills associated with change agentry. They need to know how to work outside the classroom—in the middle, with other components of the system. The concepts, ideas, and case studies in the following chapters provide a close look at grass-roots changes that were initiated by teachers, protected by wise school officials, and appreciated by communities.

Behaviors Associated with Effective Teacher-Change-Agents

In order to help you understand where this text is heading, you should have some vision of what I was thinking of when I responded to the fellow vacationer who asked me, "Who should be in charge of school reform?" When I said "teachers" I was thinking of empowered teachers like Kelly, who used her change-agentry skills to make her vision a reality. I was also thinking of many other teachers I have encountered who are expressing themselves as full-fledged professionals. For example, two successful teacher-change-agents, Ann Garrett and Suzanne Ludwig, led the way in a three-year effort to change their junior high school into a middle school. They started in September 1989 by writing a philosophy that was reviewed, revised, debated, and accepted by the faculty, the principal, and the school board in November 1989. During 1990 and 1991 they worked with fellow teachers, the administration, and the school board to make significant changes. They are now teacher leaders of faculty teams that meet weekly to plan instruction. The teams make the school schedules for students. There is a new room arrangement and a staggered-bell time schedule that eliminates congestion and reduces discipline problems that come with crowded, noisy hallways. The teams have replaced all school faculty meetings, and all memos are developed by the principal and the teachers together. They have a new parent-teacher organization that has improved home and school cooperation. There are many other positive features that exist in their school now because they had a vision and true voice that was listened to. At a recent seminar on grass-roots change, Ann and Suzanne described the key behaviors they associated with their work as change agents.

This listing represents a preview of the behaviors that support the activities described in this text. Think of this listing as a profile of what effective teacher-change-agents do as full-blown professionals. Professional teachers (Ann and Suzanne) know that if you want to fulfill the moral commitment to make a difference in the lives of your students, you need to be an effective classroom teacher and an active agent for changing the status quo. When teachers mature professionally, they:

Build credibility. First and foremost, professional teachers' credibility in the school and community shows. They have a voice and they make themselves heard. They speak up and share their ideas. They ask questions and express concerns. Furthermore, their voice has credibility because they are recognized by students, parents, teachers, and school officials as being good teachers. They have built their credibility on an authentic basis with a good work ethic and an enthusiasm for teaching.

They know how crucial good preparation is to being an effective teacher. Teachers, like all heroes, have an Achilles heel. Just as Superman has to watch out for krypton, teachers have to watch out for being unprepared. They must try to talk and act in a positive yet realistic manner, not only when they teach, but also when they work with and talk with others both in and out of school.

Participate professionally. Teachers who are change agents participate in local, state, regional, and national professional organizations. They attend meetings, often they play some leadership roles, and they read professional journals. They enjoy the educational as well as the social benefits that come from associating with other educators.

Engage in lifelong learning. Underlying change agents' participation in professional groups is their love of learning. They are excited by the prospects of finding better ways to teach. They like to do action research projects to see what happens. They read, they share ideas, and they seek to grow professionally. They have ways of gathering evidence as they teach so that they can make rational decisions about the effectiveness of materials and methods.

Interact with mentors. As lifelong learners, professional teachers know that change involves risk, so they have mentors they can talk to for ideas and for support. Mentors may be colleagues, former professors, or administrators. Having a mentoring relationship with someone is crucial. It grounds one's career and provides a context of guidance and support that is so important to continued learning and personal and professional growth.

Write and reflect. Change agents write for themselves. They keep journals and record their concerns, thoughts, and ideas. They know that the process of writing is a powerful learning device that helps them sort out problems and find solutions. They sometimes share these with others. They also write for others and seek to publish articles that disseminate good teaching practices. They like to tell their story about what works for them.

Network and communicate. Change agents have a network of other teachers whom they talk with on a regular basis. Very often such networks go beyond the local school. Belonging to professional groups is one way to build and maintain a network of colleagues. Networking, like mentoring, is important to keeping learning alive. Networking activities often include making phone calls, writing letters, trading ideas, sharing journals, and having periodic meetings. The network allows them to listen and to learn from each other.

Seek money. An interesting characteristic is the tendency of change agents to seek a variety of ways to obtain funds to buy materials, books, and teaching aids. It is no surprise that dedicated teachers spend their own money on teaching supplies and books. But change agents go further than their own pocket. They seek to influence how the principal or the school board spends money and they write grants in order to obtain support for change.

Demonstrate resiliency. Change agents are resilient and do not give up easily. When thwarted, they regroup, rewrite, develop a new strategy, and keep going. Ann said that her success at getting money and staffing to change her junior high into a middle school led some colleagues to tease that she must be having "an affair" with a school official. She said she denied this accusation with a good sense of humor and a description of how she kept going back with requests. She said, "When you try to change the status quo you can expect to hear three to five 'no's' for every 'yes.'"

Take proactive, not reactive, stances. Perhaps more than anything else, teachers who engage in successful change agentry have a proactive agenda. They do not sit back and play defense. They think, reflect, prepare, and act on their concerns. They have a vision and a plan that looks ahead, and they act in a professional manner to seek ways to make their plan work. They know that a reactive or defensive stance means that most of their time and effort will be spent putting out fires and there will be little energy left to make their vision a reality.

In this text I offer ideas, concepts, and examples that show you how these behaviors manifest themselves in teachers who effect change in school literacy programs.

Summary

This chapter introduces the idea that classroom teachers are change agents for school reform. Teachers' voices and visions are a key ingredient in changing school literacy instruction. True and lasting change occurs when teachers, bolstered by their moral purpose of making a difference in their students lives, act as change agents both individually and collectively. Historically, teachers have not been viewed as change agents, and for decades change policies and practices have come from above and outside schools. In the 1980s the realization that teachers and principals can successfully resist top-down mandates led to the current idea that true and lasting change involves collaboration and negotiation up and down and across all levels. In the 1990s we believe that the best chance for making positive changes occurs when teachers and officials work together in the middle.

Because teachers have functioned alone behind the classroom door, the idea of working in the middle, sharing in the decision making, and acting as change agents requires a new view of the role of the teacher. This new role requires new behaviors and new skills that require new training. The chapter ended with an overview of some of the basic teacher behaviors that are associated with this new role of effective change agentry. In the next chapter you will read how teachers initiate change from the grass roots.

References

Atkisson, K. (1992). *Teacher in transition.* Unpublished Master's Research Paper, Southern Illinois University, Carbondale, Ill.

Berry, B. (1986). Why bright college students won't teach. *The Urban Review, 18*(4), 269–280.

Bracey, G. W. (1991). Educational change. *Phi Delta Kappan, 72*(7), 557–560.

Darling-Hammond, L. (1988). The futures of teaching. *Educational Leadership, 43*(3), 4–10.

Darling-Hammond, L., and Berry, B. (1988). *The Evolution of Teacher Policy.* Santa Monica, Calif.: RAND Corporation.

Erickson. L. (1991). How RIPE promotes change in literacy learning in rural schools. In *Literacy: International, National, and Local.* K. Camperell and B. Hayes (Eds.), Eleventh Yearbook of the American Reading Forum, 87–95.

Farber, B. (1991). *Crisis in education.* San Francisco: Jossey-Bass.

Fiske, E. B. (1991). *Smart schools, smart kids: Why do some schools work?* New York: Simon and Schuster.

Fraatz, J. (1987). *The politics of reading.* New York: Teachers College Press.

Fullan, M. (1993). Why teachers must become change agents. *Educational Leadership, 50*(6), 12–17.

Glickman, C. (1992). Introduction: Postmodernism and supervision. In C. Glickman (Ed.) *Supervision in Transition: 1992 ASCD Yearbook.* Washington, D.C.

McClure, R. M. (1988). The evolution of shared leadership. *Educational Leadership, 46*(3), 60–62.

Meek, A. (1988). On teaching as a profession: A conversation with Linda Darling-Hammond. *Educational Leadership, 46*(3), 11–17.

Pearson, P. D. (1992). RT remembrance: The second 20 years. *The Reading Teacher, 45,* 378–385.

Pearson, L. C., and Hall, B. W. (1993). Initial construct validity of the teaching autonomy scale. *Journal of Educational Research, 86*(3), 172-178.

Stedman, L., and Smith, M. (1983). Recent reform proposals for American education. Reprinted in Dougherty, K., and Hammack, F. (1990). *Education and society.* New York: Harcourt Brace Jovanovich. 642–667.

2

How Teachers
Initiate Change

*When it comes to considering change, the opinions
that matter most to teachers are likely those
of their charges, not their peers.** *

When visiting schools, I have learned to ask teachers to draw me a detailed map that shows me how to find their school. Recently I visited a school to talk about an integrated reading and writing environmental science program, and the map and directions said, "Turn right at John Deere after you cross the railroad tracks." This detailed information was exactly what I needed and I found the school without much trouble.

In a similar fashion this chapter and the ones that follow are maps that may guide teachers when they seek to improve their reading and writing programs. And just as a map is merely a visual representation, and an aid for future travelers, this chapter is only a representation of the real tasks faced by a faculty trying to make improvements. But remember, good mapmakers get their information firsthand and report what they actually see—so think of this chapter as a map of what I have observed.

When you consider the ideas in this chapter, I want you to remember that there are many excellent school reading programs that should be maintained, fine-tuned, and supported. All schools do not need a major overhaul. All schools do not need to implement whole language pro-

---

*Robert L. Larson, 1992. *Changing Schools from the Inside Out*, p. 34.

19

grams, nor do all schools need to implement skill-oriented programs. This book and this chapter do not endorse one philosophy of reading and writing over another. Instead, I want you to focus on how teachers initiate and implement whatever changes they believe will improve literacy learning.

What Can We Learn from Watching Teachers?

About ten years ago, in a one-week time span, consulting trips took me to rural Appalachia and the urban east. Expecting to see differences, I was struck by the classroom similarities in tiny Wallace, West Virginia, and the affluent Washington-Baltimore suburb of Columbia, Maryland. Of course Columbia was newer, richer, and appeared more up-to-date. But geographic, architectural, economic, and obvious social differences that mark communities do not automatically cause great differences in what teachers do with children of similar age and developmental levels. The second grade teacher in the heart of the bituminous coal belt didn't have the new furniture and the video camera taping equipment like the teacher in the suburbs. But both teachers had to say and do just about the same things to get their young students reading and writing. They also had similar classroom routines that fit with what second graders do, wherever they live. As I said, it would be nice to report significant differences in rural and urban classrooms, but my observations revealed little difference in what we might expect to happen in reading and writing in both settings. The most striking differences between old and new classrooms are ceilings and floors—warped wood compared to smooth carpeting, and dim globe lights in contrast to bright fluorescent lighting. Meanwhile, the walls in both places are very similar. Second grade walls are covered with children's drawings and writings that have an uncanny sameness. I have seen more variance within a single school (no matter where it is) than there is between rural and urban settings. But if this is so, then what is there to learn by looking at schools? Simply this—most of the school-improvement research is based on urban schools. That is fine, I have no argument with that. But I have found rural schools to be excellent places to observe how bottom-up grass-roots changes in literacy learning occur. In rural schools there are fewer consultants and specialists, so teacher watchers like me have an opportunity to report on how individual and small groups of classroom teachers go about improving literacy learning on their own. School watching in America, whether it be in town or in the country, has convinced me that true change is a teacher-by-teacher, grass-roots affair. And whether the school is rural or urban is not the issue. In the next section I will explain this further.

Some Features of Grass-Roots or Bottom-Up Change

Although one-third of all teachers in the United States work in rural areas, most school improvement studies have reported on teachers in urban and suburban schools. Some writers say that what works for larger schools with central office curriculum consultants may not work in rural settings (DeYoung, 1987). Is this because the rural schools have less access to consultants? This used to be my own bias. But now, based on my experiences in both rural and urban schools, I am convinced that a teacher-based grass-roots approach will work regardless of where the school is. I am not suggesting that central office specialists are not important. But I am saying that consultants are most effective when they work to facilitate grass-roots approaches to improving the teaching of reading and writing. Even if you are a central office consultant in an urban district, you will need to approach change from the bottom up.

For example, even though rural teachers do not have easy access to specialists, there are other features that provide advantages that can aid in school improvement (National School Boards Association, 1987). Usually there is a low teacher-pupil ratio, a high degree of teacher autonomy, a chance to work with a small, close-knit group of teachers, and high parental and community involvement. In addition, teachers in rural settings tend to experience a variety of teaching assignments over time. On the other hand, we know that rural teachers face some disadvantages, such as personal and professional isolation. And sometimes they may teach several grade levels as well as coach or supervise extracurricular activities. Also, teaching outside their areas of greatest comfort and competence is not uncommon, because they are likely to be moved to other teaching assignments when student class sizes change (Killian and Byrd, 1988). But these disadvantages are often offset by other factors that help teachers to initiate change. Some of these factors are: a long-term commitment to their jobs as well as close personal ties to the community; credibility with the parents; and a small school workplace that enables them to interact more closely with their colleagues. These factors are important for two reasons: (1) They reveal several conditions that allow school-improvement efforts to succeed (Huberman and Crandall, 1983); and (2) They reveal that improving the teaching of reading and writing is basically a bottom-up or grass-roots effort—in other words, a teacher-centered process. In a similar fashion other writers such as Larson (1991) report "Typically teachers—not principals—initiated [small scale] innovations. The principals supported the improvements, but they rarely "told" their staffs to change (p. 551)."

Teachers Are the Change Agents

It is true that teachers in rural settings are also less likely to have access to central office consultants and are likely to be ". . . left much to themselves to look for solutions to problems and for ways of acquiring new skills or training" (Killian and Byrd, 1988, p. 38). While this is usually cited as a disadvantage, it may be just the opposite. The idea of teacher helping teacher has been found to be more effective than coaching by an outside trainer (Sparks, 1986). And teachers have reported that their best source of new ideas are often other teachers (Roberts, 1982). And while it may be that small schools may have an advantage, in that important school improvement collegial arrangements may be easier to organize, larger schools have found ways to bring teachers together. The point is that even with central office specialists, or quick access to local colleges or universities, the fact is that change is basically an individual and personal affair for teachers. In his *Phi Delta Kappan* research column, Bracey (1991) reports that two decades of school reform have shown us that what matters most is not top-down policy or what is rational from a data-driven perspective. Instead, he says that local choices about whether to change and how to implement a policy are more important than funding, governance, program design, and technology. He goes on to say that teacher networks and informal groups are more powerful arrangements than formal policies from the top (district and state) down to the school and classroom. The following cartoon illustrates what teachers have been doing with top-down policies for a long time.

The need for a smallness and a closeness is so important that this feature alone can be more advantageous than access to outside help. The cardinal rule of bottom-up change could be: The smaller the number of participants, the more effective the change. As a former COSOB (Central Office SOB), I can personally attest to the limited help teachers and principals often get from curriculum specialists! I hope you don't misunderstand me. I am not against consultants. My point is that, whether you have central office consultants or state- and university-based experts, they are best used when they are controlled by the true change agents— the teachers. The fact that I have made reference to rural examples is not to say that small schools are better. Rather, the absence of central office or other outside "change agents" has only allowed me to highlight and authenticate the power that teachers have for being change agents.

FIGURE 2-1

Used by permission of Jim Hall.

Teachers As Literacy Leaders

While leadership is a crucial issue there is a danger in raising leadership issues over literacy. The current general belief in America is that literacy levels are too low and someone is to blame. The rhetoric of blame causes us to seek quick fixes, simple answers, and top-down mandates about testing teachers and raising standards. In reality we sense that although leadership for improving literacy is a responsibility that is shared by both school and community, we must look inside the school. When we do, we see a shared leadership pattern between the principal and teachers.

For example, in a study (Erickson, 1991) of teachers who attended the Renewal Institute for Practicing Educators (RIPE), we looked at changes they made in their teaching of reading and writing. One part of the research examined the relationship between RIPE teachers and their principals. It was very much like the model of teacher empowerment described by Maeroff (1988) and Larson (1991), in that teachers assume responsibility for instructional policies without disrupting the role of the principal. Both teachers and principals seem to be comfortable with the active and autonomous role that teachers play in determining and implementing changes in reading and writing instruction. Very often individual or small groups of teachers implement ideas on their own. When asked about this they often say the principal "leaves me alone" or "she wouldn't object" or "I don't feel as though I need to consult my principal when I try out a new idea." The exception to this is when a change requires money. For example, when RIPE teachers made changes in their reading instruction they reported good administrative support and approval to use reading workbook money to buy sets of children's literature books. Another aspect of teacher leadership for improving reading and writing, revealed in the same study, is the interesting perception of collegial support among elementary teachers. When asked to give specific examples of collegial support, teachers almost always mentioned another single teacher, either in their school or from another school, who often listened to them and provided alternate ideas when problems occurred. Another aspect of collegial support is the tendency for teachers to give each other room to make changes without giving overt help. One teacher told of how her fellow teachers shifted recess times and loaned her books to help her increase her sustained silent reading plan, although they themselves did not adopt the idea or talk to her much about the activity. Therefore, part of the picture that emerges regarding leadership is that many teachers are more interested in tending their own garden than they are in widespread land reform (Huberman, 1989, p. 51), and new reading and writing practices are for the most part implemented by individual teachers—with and without principal support.

To summarize, teachers tend to assume responsibility for changing reading and writing instruction without disrupting the role of the principal. Principals and teachers appear comfortable with the active and autonomous role teachers play. And new ideas travel beyond the classroom walls in a natural fashion as students, teachers, principals, and parents share their positive reactions with others. This suggests that leadership for improving literacy learning may be less mysterious and difficult to develop than is often thought. For example, instead of literacy leadership training programs for principals or other "change agents" it may be wiser to go directly to experienced teachers. The goal is to provide them with relevant learning experiences and create "learning communities" where individual teachers link together. To illustrate this point the following section describes a recent bottom-up literacy-improvement effort that teachers directed in two adjacent small towns in Southern Illinois (Hileman, 1990).

A Case Study Example

When I asked Linda to tell her story she said, "I tried to tell it just like I was talking to my mother." Here is Linda's story of how she changed school and family reading practices.

> As a project in a graduate reading class I was taking with Dr. Erickson, and after reading *Becoming a Nation of Readers* (1985), Mary Ann and I decided to use the book's 17 recommendations to poll teachers in our two elementary schools. We asked the principals and teachers to select the recommendations they felt were most important for im-

proving reading. After tallying the results we were surprised to see that both schools chose the same four top items. Encouraged by this initial response and by some excited talk in the teachers' lounge, we decided to have the principals and teachers rank in order the top seven items from the first poll. We found that the overwhelming choice supported the need for more parent involvement and more independent reading by the children.

The interest that these activities created among the staff prompted me to ask the principal if I could make a presentation at the November faculty meeting about what action they might take based upon the survey results. So I talked with other teachers and we planned a meeting that, in addition to refreshments, would include a discussion of what to do to promote parent involvement and more independent reading. Because I was reluctant to lead a large group I asked Dr. Erickson and Dr. Killian to help me guide the discussion. Both professors presented short descriptions and shared materials that told what other schools in the area were doing with parents and independent reading. During the discussion and in response to the question "What do we do now?" Dr. Erickson suggested that the school form a steering committee to plan school activities that would involve parents and increase reading at home. Several teachers asked questions about problems and successes other schools were experiencing and several expressed interest in exploring the idea. The meeting ended with small groups talking while they snacked on hot cider and doughnuts.

The next week I placed a note in every mailbox asking for volunteers to serve on a steering committee, and I was pleased when 15 of the 27 responded "yes." In early December 11 teachers met and we decided that, in addition to ideas for teachers and parents, we needed money for reading improvement. So I wrote to the superintendent asking him to inform the school board of the group's desire to work on reading improvement. The superintendent and the board agreed that teachers could have $25 each for books and novel units. At the same time two other teachers wrote a grant and received $700 to buy novels for class study and independent reading. With this initial enthusiasm and support the steering committee continued to meet monthly. To keep interest and in the hope of gaining more support, I distributed the minutes of the meetings to everyone in the school. During these initial meetings, in the winter and early spring, the teachers not only discussed parent involvement, but found it very easy and natural to share ideas about new ways to teach reading and writing.

All of this renewed interest in methods made me curious about what was happening in our classrooms. So before the April meeting I distributed a questionnaire to see what new strategies the teachers had been using. I knew that some teachers enrolled in reading classes at the university were in touch with new ideas, but I was surprised that the teachers reported using 54 new activities during the year so far. The most valuable activities, according to the teachers, were the teacher reading aloud to students and sustained silent reading in class. In addition, 14 teachers reported that they would like to see an all-school activity involving at-home reading. As school wound down in May, the superintendent told me about an upcoming training session at the regional educational service center, which she and another teacher attended. The presentation was through the National Diffusion Network and it described an all-school reading-for-enjoyment program called *Books and Beyond*. It was a great idea, and I said, "This is just what we are looking for." The manual for the program was $40, and as luck would have it, a fellow teacher won the door prize which allowed us to purchase it for half price! As school ended we promised to keep going during the summer.

At a summer meeting at my house nine teachers gathered, and I explained the *Books and Beyond* program. Everyone agreed it would be appropriate at our schools. In the fall we got money and time from the administration to present the program to the entire school staff. The staff was excited and agreed to participate in a two-hour workshop with a speaker from the National Diffusion Network, in November 1989. All of this coincided with another school-parent involvement activity led by the superintendent, as well as support from the regional educational service center, which agreed to pay for the NDN speaker. Following the program, 22 teachers agreed to work on one of the four committees that would implement the program in January 1990 and run it until May. As I look back, I find that this has been a personally rewarding experience. The amazing aspect of this change in our reading program has been the cooperation and exchange between teachers. Prior to this we had little idea what the teacher next door to us was doing. Now we are planning idea-exchanging meetings each month for math, too! I have appreciated expressions of gratitude from everyone involved. Perhaps my greatest surprise was receiving a copy of a letter my principal sent to the superintendent and board congratulating me on our exciting activities. I have taught for 12 years now, and this is the first formal letter of recognition I have ever received.

The *Books and Beyond* program lasted from January through May of 1990, and one feature of the program involved recording the amounts of each child's book reading on a large chart called Jog Across America. Prizes were awarded for reading, and over 200 students won tickets to Six Flags amusement park by reading halfway across America. Other prizes that were awarded for different amounts of reading included: medals, school pizza parties, a cassette deck, movie and gift passes, and certificates from Illinois and United States senators. I also spoke to parent groups and was interviewed by the newspaper and two radio stations. Parent volunteers were recruited to keep records and teachers even competed.

When I tabulated the responses from parents and other records I found that over 80 people in the community (parents, business owners, service organizations) helped at school, donated money, or contributed prizes. The community librarian reported that February and March were the busiest months on record. Three times as many students visited the community library in February and March than in October and November. The number of books checked out by students increased from an average 187 per month in October-November to 544 per month in February-March. Parents also reported that TV viewing time decreased and reading at home time increased. Ninety-two percent of the primary grade parents, 86 percent of the grade three-to-five parents, and 60 percent of the grade six-to-eight parents said they would like the program repeated.

As I reflect on all of the work and the positive community response, I have found that this project has helped me to realize that teachers have the power to change what occurs at home, to some extent. Parent comments in church, at the grocery store, and at school proved this to me time and time again.

Some Comments on Linda's Story

An important point to consider is that Linda's story spans two years. And while her attempts to make reading more enjoyable were successful, they were marked by a host of delays and conflicts. The truth is that successful change is fraught with frustrating events that create never-ending problems. What sustained Linda and the other teachers was their concern for students. They truly wanted to make reading more enjoyable for the children. This concern for the children is the most powerful source of energy for driving change.

But how did Linda deal with problems? This is not a simple question to answer, so the next chapter will discuss how teachers and principals deal with the conflicts and barriers that inevitably accompany attempts to improve. Before we do that we need to take a closer look at how Linda and Mary Ann started the dialogue that led to the increase in enjoyable reading at school and in the community. Their approach involved surveying the teachers and principals at their schools, summarizing the results, and calling a meeting (the cider and doughnut session) to share the results.

BOX 2-1

We are interested in learning what the teachers in the district feel are the most vital to them. Please take a few minutes to read these recommendations. After reading them, please go back and mark the five that you feel are the most important. Also check the grade level or class you presently work with. We plan to summarize the results and report back to you. Please return the survey to Linda by October 14. Thank you for your cooperation.

Reading Survey

__Elementary (K-3)   __Middle (4-5)   __Jr. High (6-8)
__"Special" Teacher   __Administrator

1. Parents should read to preschool children and informally teach them about reading and writing.
2. Parents should support school-aged children's continued growth as readers.
3. Preschool and kindergarten reading readiness programs should focus on reading, writing, and oral language.
4. Teachers should maintain classrooms that are both stimulating and disciplined.
5. Teachers of beginning reading should present well-designed phonics instruction.
6. Reading primers should be interesting, comprehensible, and give children opportunities to apply phonics.
7. Teachers should devote more time to comprehension instruction.
8. Children should spend less time completing workbooks and skill sheets.
9. Children should spend more time in independent reading.
10. Children should spend more time writing.
11. Textbooks should contain adequate explanations of important concepts.
12. Schools should cultivate an ethos (environment and attitudes) that supports reading.
13. Schools should maintain well-stocked and managed libraries.
14. Schools should introduce more comprehensive assessments of reading and writing.
15. Schools should attract and hold more able teachers.
16. Teacher education programs should be lengthened and improved in quality.
17. Schools should provide for the continuing professional development of teachers.

Surveying the Staff

One way to seek support for a literacy improvement project is to ask everyone at school for their opinion. For example, Linda and Mary Ann developed a survey and a cover letter based on the 17 recommendations from the book *Becoming a Nation of Readers* (1985). Their cover letter and survey looked like the one in Box 2-1.

Summarizing and Sharing the Results

In order to promote interest and stimulate and satisfy curiosity it is important to report back promptly to the staff with all of the results. Responses were counted and the following sample of results were distributed back to everyone (even those who did not respond). For example, they found that the staff concerns centered on four items. Here is how they reported back to the teachers:

> *Thanks for returning your questionnaires. We gave out 35 and the twenty-seven people who responded (77%) included 8 from K–3, 4 from 4–5, 6 from 6–8, 7 from special classes, and 2 principals. The highest-rated items included:*
>
> > *1 Parents should read to children and informally teach them about reading and writing. [This was checked by 20 people]*
> > *2 Parents should support school-aged children's continued growth as readers. [This was checked by 16 people]*
> > *4 Teachers should maintain stimulating and well-disciplined classrooms. [This was checked by 16 people]*
> > *9 Children should spend more time in independent reading. [This was checked by 14 people]*

These and the results of all of the responses to all items were distributed to the staff, and this caused a lot of discussion throughout the school. The next step was to call a meeting and ask for volunteers to meet and discuss the results in the hopes of forming some type of ad hoc group that would make plans for dealing with the top concerns. As Linda described in her story, the meeting led to a core of people who decided to work together to plan activities that promoted independent reading, both in school and in the homes of the students.

Reflecting on Getting Started

The key to initiating this schoolwide program was the way dialogue was stimulated from a proactive stance. Certainly there is plenty of reactive dialogue in schools. Just listen to a typical teacher-lounge conversation about the never-ending problems and conflicts that exist in all schools. The important point here is that teachers lead the way by carrying out action research like the survey activity we have just described. Linda and Mary Ann developed a proactive agenda that attempted to get people to talk about a positive direction they were willing to take to promote reading for enjoyment for their students. This type of dialogue is distinctly different from the all-too-typical reactive complaining that exists in all workplaces.

Other ways to stimulate proactive dialogue instead of surveys include small group interviews. Sometimes teachers prefer to talk and discuss instead of writing, so a series of informal interviews are carried out with all of the staff. To facilitate this, two to five teachers from similar grade levels meet and discuss several questions while ideas are tape-recorded or written down by a recorder. Sometimes a chalkboard or a flip chart is used to capture key points. Results from these interviews are put into a report format and distributed to every staff member. Then a meeting (voluntary) is scheduled to discuss the results and get some commitment to proceed.

Another plan is have a demonstration video of a classroom using an effective reading strategy, or a respected and articulate teacher can present a program. Immediately after watching and listening to the presentation, small groups of teachers can discuss what they witnessed and list ideas that they might want to pursue. These ideas can be put into a report and distributed to the staff. Again, the next step is to call a meeting (again— you guessed it—volunteers) and attempt to get some commitment to proceed.

Summary

Teachers are ideal informal leaders. Linda and Mary Ann initiated dialogue across the entire staff by using a survey. They summarized and shared data from the survey and called a meeting to discuss the results. This led to an agreement to take some action. They formed an improvement committee that worked over a two-year period to initiate successful changes within the school and in the community. The key to this was having two teachers take the lead by asking all teachers to respond to a questionnaire. This enabled a significant group (27 of 35 staff members) to generate their own lists of concerns, which were the agenda for the first meeting of volunteers. At the first meeting ideas were discussed and clarified and examples of other successful activities were shared. There was enough concern to get some commitment from the staff to proceed to plan activities that involved the community. There was enough energy generated to sustain a two-year project that dealt with these concerns. This chapter portrayed teachers who acted as literacy leaders in their school and community. The next chapter presents a realistic look at the perils that accompany change and provides ideas for dealing with conflicts and obstacles as they arise.

References

Becoming a nation of readers: The report of the commission on reading. (1985). Washington, D.C.: National Institute of Education.

Bracey, G. W. (March 1991). Educational change. *Phi Delta Kappan, 72,* 557–560.

DeYoung, A. J. (1987). The status of American rural education research: An integrated review and commentary. *Review of Educational Research, 57,* 123–148.

Erickson, L. (1991). How RIPE promotes change in literacy learning in rural schools. In Hayes, B., and Camperell, K. (Eds), *Literacy: International, national, state, and local.* Yearbook of the American Reading Forum, Vol. XI, 87–95.

Hileman, L. (1990). *Reading for enjoyment project.* Unpublished research paper. Southern Illinois University, Carbondale, Ill.

Huberman, M. (1989). The professional life cycle of teachers. *Teachers College Record, 91,* 31–57.

Huberman, M., and Crandall, D. (1983). *People, policies, and practices: Examining the chain of school improvement.* In Vol. 9: Implications for Action, A Study of Dissemination Efforts Supporting School Improvement. Andover, Mass.: The Network.

Killian, J. E., and Byrd, D. M. (Fall 1988). A cooperative staff development model that taps the strengths of rural schools. *Journal of Staff Development, 9,* 34–39.

Larson, R. L. (March 1991). Small is beautiful: Innovation from the inside out. *Phi Delta Kappan, 72,* 550–554.

Larson, R. L. (1992). *Changing schools from the inside out.* Lancaster, Pa.: Technomic Publishing Co.

Maeroff, G.I. (1988). *The empowerment of teachers: Overcoming the crisis of confidence.* New York: Teachers College Press.

National School Boards Association, (1987). *Good teachers: An unblinking look at supply and preparedness.* Washington, D.C.: National School Boards Association. (Monograph #1 in the series, Today's Issues in Education, by Susan Hooper.)

Roberts, N. (1982). *Adult learner characteristics and learning styles.* Charleston: West Virginia Bureau of Learning Systems.

Sparks, G.M. (1986). The effectiveness of alternative training activities in changing teaching practices. *American Educational Research Journal, 23,* 217–225.

3

_____

Overcoming Obstacles and Conflicts

Obstacles can arise regardless of the type of change or of the approach taken to support the change.*

Teachers like Linda who successfully lead others in changing the status quo encounter conflicts. This chapter is a primer on dealing with a variety of obstacles, conflicts, or gaps that thwart school improvement. My intent is to present some basic information about planned change, adult learning, and school arrangements that support efforts to improve student learning in reading and writing. The ideas, processes, and practices that are presented in this chapter are aimed at helping teachers and principals become better at dealing with conflicts or gaps that inevitably accompany school improvement initiatives.

The major point of this chapter is that successful change activities, such as meetings, discussions, decisions, and even the development of materials, are best conceived in response to specific gaps and conflicts that arise along the way. Waiting until conflicts cease is a naive posture that is simply wrong. The fact of the matter is that the potholes that plague change cannot be ignored or eliminated. They are always in the way. Successful change always involves using change tactics for slowing down and going over rough spots. For example, consider the problem Jean encountered and notice how strategies were selected in response to the barriers she perceived.

_____

*Douglas Carnine, 1988. *How to Overcome Barriers to Student Achievement*, p. 62.

A pothole for Jean was her concern that new practices for teaching reading comprehension would mean that she might spend up to three days on one story and therefore she would never finish all the stories and activities in the book for her grade level. Jean was caught between her old practice of completing the reading text and the new practice of selecting stories that would allow her to help students practice and apply comprehension strategies. In Jean's words, "The idea of skipping some stories and workbook pages was like asking me to agree to adultery." The way around this pothole was a series of meetings over a period of two months in which the principal, Jean, and the other teachers agreed that it was not necessary to cover all the stories and workbook pages in order to achieve the school literacy goals. This agreement marked a huge step in closing the gap between many current school reading practices and promising new teaching ideas.

Change As Gap Reduction

In schools, change means "becoming better" or "closing the gap" between what we image as "ideal" reading and writing instruction and what we are presently doing. Gap reduction is a powerful and useful concept because it allows us to keep a firm grasp on the relationship between various strategies for change and the fundamental goals for change, such as those described in *Becoming a Nation of Readers* (1985). For example, changes can close gaps but they might also cause conflict because other results of the change are not valued. Such was the case reported by Shannon (1986) when administrators mandated a plan that featured standardized teaching plus merit pay. This approach did improve reading achievement scores. However, some teachers adopted a test-score view of reading; others complained that teaching reading was less fulfilling; some principals applied intolerable pressure, and a few teachers cheated on the test to obtain merit. The point of course is that, ideally, changes ought to lead to outcomes that are considered valuable by everyone (teachers, students, administrators, parents) with a stake in the school. But they often don't and conflict occurs.

Change Brings Conflict

One of the reasons that change and conflict go hand in hand is that different images of the ideal exist. What is your image of an ideal reader? What is your image of an ideal classroom reading/writing lesson or the ideal content area reading lesson or the ideal school reading program?

Images of the ideal literate student and the outcomes actually achieved by students are really the two edges of the gap, which we hope to reduce by changing something in the system. In schools the gap between ideal reading images and actual outcomes is addressed by curriculum guidelines that assign sets of goals and objectives to different grades and different content areas. Very often conflict that is associated with change is due to a lack of agreement, not only about goals and objectives but also about the means to reach these images. Another source of conflict is that change often threatens to alter roles, relationships, and responsibilities of adults who make up the school system. In addition, images of the ideal change over time, so the gaps can widen and current teaching efforts can be outstripped by social change. Such is the case for increased literacy demands in an information age. And so for all of us who teach reading and writing, change not only involves managing conflicts; it also means that instead of closing the gap between the current and the ideal, it is more realistic to seek to reduce it—or at least keep it from widening.

The Big Picture of Change

In order for teachers and principals to get a better grasp of what can be done to maximize change and reduce conflict, Box 3-1 (adapted from Leithwood, 1986) is presented as a "big picture" that maps the significant features of change. The intent of the following discussion is to stand back and examine the entire context for change. This should help us to better understand the complex relationships of shared agreements, which is necessary if gaps between the current and ideal are to be reduced. It may also help us chart a course through the ever-present mine field of conflicts. Finally, this view provides a "semantic map" of the significant features of change that will have to be considered as teachers and principals move toward common reading ideals. The significant features of the "Big Picture" that will be considered are: (1) Stages of Change; (2) The System; and (3) Obstacles, Conflicts and Change Strategies. Feature 1, Stages of Change, refers to the process of growing from a current status to a desired or ideal state that is envisioned as the "ideal." Feature 2, The System, refers to the staff, the materials, the practices, and all of the components that comprise the status quo. The third feature refers to the obstacles and/or conflicts that will arise along the way, as well as the change strategies that are selected to overcome these barriers. All of these components must be viewed as a whole when we expect to make changes.

One implication of this large picture of change is that all parts of the system are connected. For example, in order to help students reach desired levels of literacy demanded by society, we cannot change just one

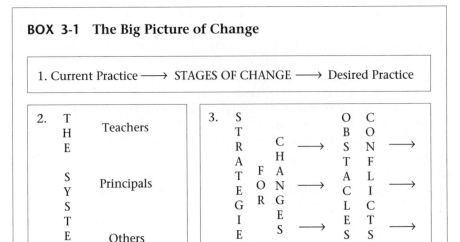

BOX 3-1   The Big Picture of Change

1. Current Practice ⟶ STAGES OF CHANGE ⟶ Desired Practice

feature of the literacy curriculum. Change in one part means change in another. Changing texts may affect grading practices, which in turn affects parents, which in turn affects parent-teacher conferences, and on and on.

The most important implication of this big picture of change is that strategies must be selected on the basis of their potential for overcoming specific obstacles. This is so important that it will be discussed in more detail in the next section. School personnel who are competent and successful as change agents understand how these three key components—stages of change, the system, and obstacles/conflicts and strategies for change—are all related. What follows is a basic primer on current theory and practice in change agentry. The discussion is organized around each of the three components from Box 3-1. Understanding each of these concepts, as well as their relationship to each other, is crucial if teachers and principals intend to successfully implement change.

1. Stages of Change

Adult change is gradual, and rarely do teachers and principals dramatically shift behaviors in a short period of time. In addition, adults do not change unless they actively control the learning situation and are intrinsically motivated to move through learning stages (Andrews, Houston, Bryant, 1981). Successful change activities feature active adult involvement from the very beginning of the change cycle. The trick is to skillfully match strategies to the "growth" pattern that adults follow as they move from one stage to the next to achieve a desired behavior. In the following section each growth stage (Erickson, 1982) is briefly described and followed by sample strategies.

Awareness-Interest Stage

A new idea is acknowledged rather passively at first and a general opinion, either positive or negative, is formed about the change. At this stage brief, positive, *attention-getting tactics* are effective, such as short questionnaires and small action-research activities. An early activity is to have the adults generate the data or ideas for initial discussions by having them write down and discuss their opinions and feelings about a current reading/writing issue. A good rule to remember was aptly put by one adult, who said, "Unless we know it already, we're not interested." In chapter one, we saw how Linda and Mary Ann used a survey to do this.

Mental-Tryout Stage

Adults imagine the idea in their own situation and decide whether it is worth an actual tryout. *Show-and-tell tactics* testifying to the worth and success of a new idea are effective at this stage. When participants say, "Has it worked any other place?" case studies, audiovisual aids, or recorded interviews of satisfied users are effective. Again, the first meeting that Linda and Mary Ann arranged featured some show-and-tell about what other schools were doing to involve parents and the community in reading for enjoyment.

Trial and Adoption Stage

When adults alter old practices or try new ideas they begin on a cautious and temporary basis, they see what happens, and if they are satisfied they continue to use the idea. Through a process of integration and adaptation of materials, what was once just an idea can eventually become a regular routine. When teachers and principals seek materials, guidance, and a chance to try an idea, *training tactics* are used to guide and support initial tryouts. Sometimes an excellent teacher educator demonstrates a new technique, although in most cases an experienced teacher is the best trainer. Specific dates, times, materials, and equipment are available to support tryouts. Small groups of teachers and principals meet frequently to plan, discuss problems, share successes, coach each other, and seek help. Informal social activities are held to give everyone a chance to share experiences, receive recognition.

School personnel who understand that they cannot simply engineer changes realize that a new idea can be rejected at any point in these stages. They also realize that individuals experience the stages at different rates. And skipping over, ignoring, changing the order, or hurrying through the process can guarantee conflict. For example, teachers will resist the use of trade books if a training session is held before teachers have had a chance to do a mental tryout, ask questions, or clarify concerns. And if no modeling or trial teaching with peer support is provided, teachers will likely reject attempts to change the way they ask questions. Ignoring the stages of change that accompany adult learning is a major source of conflict. In order to overcome this potential barrier to change, it is necessary to understand how the school as a "system" thwarts change.

2. Changing the System

Because roles and relationships in schools are linked in a collective fashion, proposed changes in reading programs and reading instruction are actually changes in the "system." For example, when approached to change from a basal-reader approach to a "real book" and whole language approach in her fourth grade, Jean is, in effect, changing her role. Her new role contains some unknowns, so she will have questions for other teachers and her principal. This specific change has implications for her classroom discipline, the use of new materials, the use of the school library, the district testing program, the report card, and parent expectations. In short, if Jean is to successfully change there will have to be changes or adjustments in the system of working conditions that surround her.

An important feature of school systems that may both help and hurt Jean's effort to change is what research (Weik, 1976) describes as "loose coupling." Studies show that teachers work in relative isolation, and teachers, schools, and boards tend to function rather independently. This may help Jean in that she may be able to make some changes on her own without disturbing other teachers. Some researchers (Fraatz, 1987) who have examined this issue believe that teachers are ". . . currently the preeminent wielders of power in public schools" (p. 191). On the other hand, the combination of "loose coupling" and isolation has led teachers to feel powerless about making changes to improve student outcomes. This means that in the current system principals have at best an indirect and rather weak role in that they ". . . consent to the teacher's exercise of power and influence" (Fraatz, 1987, p. 192). At best they may only effect change in students through a loose process of negotiation and persuasion with classroom teachers, who may or may not feel empowered to attempt change.

Thus, the gap between the current and the ideal remains open unless "the system" becomes more tightly coupled so that the teachers' power is coupled or shared with other teachers and the principal. Much of the current literature on successful change activities deals with how "loose" coupling is "tightened" when new arrangements in the system allow teachers and principals to join together to reflect collectively, share decision making, and assist each other in moving toward common ideals.

The implication is that everyone must work together to nurture changes in the everyday working conditions in order to assist Jean and others to change what goes on in classrooms. Research strongly suggests that, in addition to focusing solely on individual teachers like Jean, the school culture needs to reduce teacher isolation, and the responsibility and capacity to plan instruction must be ". . . extended to educators other than classroom teachers" (Fraatz, 1987, p. 200). A review of the research on school improvement shows that the most successful change was built on a foundation of "collaboration and cooperation, involving provisions for people to do things together, talking together, and sharing concerns" (Lieberman and Miller, 1984, p. 16). This is being achieved in rural schools when principals and teachers form school-based reading-improvement teams that plan, guide, and support Jean, and of course each other, through the stages of change. Very often this team approach represents a new organizational arrangement that goes a long way to help overcome the isolation that breeds obstacles and conflicts that thwart change.

3. Obstacles/Conflicts and Change Strategies

Change or growth is not only linked to stages of change in individuals and changes in the system. Growth is also dependent upon how precisely a given change strategy is able to overcome a host of obstacles. For example, as Jean moves through the stages and mentally imagines altering her use of the basal reader, she will be concerned about her own skills, her students' achievement, classroom discipline, the need for new books, and the principal's and other teachers' opinions. These and other potential obstacles will not be overcome by a single in-service or videotape on a whole language approach to reading. Jean will be helped if she is able to raise these concerns with other teachers and the principal early in the change cycle. And her path to implementing the change will be helped if she and the principal work together to select training strategies that are designed to overcome specific obstacles during the trial and adoption stages. Research (Leithwood, 1986) and practice suggest several major sources of obstacles.

1. Lack of knowledge or skill.
2. Lack of peer support and trust.

3. Lack of incentive, reward, or motivation.
4. Lack of material resources.
5. Lack of appropriate organizational arrangements.

One way to design training strategies that overcome obstacles and conflicts is for teachers and principals to list perceived obstacles. To do this, make a list in response to the following question: What obstacles do you foresee that may prevent you from implementing a change, such as direct instruction in metacognitive strategies or whole language units, in your classroom? Sharing and discussing obstacles and conflicts at the beginning of the change process helps increase the chances that successful change strategies will be selected. Of course, many conflicts cannot be forecast at the onset. Unexpected obstacles that inevitably arise along the way are best handled by open and candid discussion. The following discussion (Erickson, 1981) of how change strategies are matched to obstacles and conflicts is not exhaustive but serves to illustrate some ways to proceed.

Lack of Knowledge and Skill

When teachers and principals say "we don't know how" it helps to use strategies such as observation of other teachers, role playing, micro-teaching, guided practice, buddy systems, and peer coaching. Sometimes the use of a written script with student handouts is a good idea in the beginning stages of practicing a new teaching skill. Plenty of support and immediate feedback from colleagues and a long try-out period are also essential to overcoming the "I don't know how" obstacle.

Lack of Support and Trust

This barrier is often stated in a "they won't let me" form. Perhaps because of the isolated nature of their work, teachers may perceive other teachers, the principal, or parents as obstacles to change. One way to deal with this concern is to arrange a meeting at which these claims are discussed openly. Often such a strategy reveals that this conflict is more imagined than real. On the other hand, frank discussions often show the need for clarity, and agreements are reached only after some intense negotiation. In any case the tendency to think that others, in or out of the system, are obstacles to change is best handled by candid discussion. One of the interesting outcomes of these discussions is often a new trust among former adversaries. At the risk of oversimplifying, consider that trust is enhanced when adults (teachers, parents, principals) can predict each other's reactions to new goals, objectives, and teaching activities. The key idea in this definition of trust is *prediction*. For, in order to predict each other's responses, the adults need to communicate often and openly.

Trust is built between adults when they experience repeated success at predicting each other's reactions in both good and bad situations.

Lack of Reward

Change is hard work that requires a significant amount of sustained energy. And there is no guarantee that early efforts will be productive. Therefore, it is important to plan change activities that include social rewards, such as food, entertainment, and pleasant working conditions. In addition to salary, college credit, and released time, it is important to arrange intrinsic rewards, such as media publicity and other forms of recognition. And while these rewards are basic to sustaining initial change activities, teachers report that long-range satisfaction and sustained motivation came from students, parents, and the community.

Lack of Material Support

Every time teachers are asked to think about obstacles and conflicts, it's a good bet they will mention lack of time, money, materials, and administrative support. These organizational obstacles can be reduced somewhat by having reading-improvement teams of teachers, supervisors, and administrators that jointly negotiate time lines, budgets, materials, and work assignments. Some schools have reduced conflict by giving these teams direct control over money for consultants, materials, and other resources. A good rule of thumb (Erickson, 1987) is to spend 80 percent on local teachers and principals and 20 percent on consultants and others from outside the school. Instead of lavishing funds on big-name visitors, the money is kept at home to send teachers and principals to workshops and courses. And some schools pay stipends to local outstanding teachers when they lead sessions and teach and coach other teachers through the stages of change. Another good policy is to make funds available for teachers to buy the materials they need. Finally, only competent and effective outside speakers are used, and they come only when and where it is convenient for the local staff.

Lack of Organizational Arrangements

For the most part schools are much better organized to run than they are organized to change. Teachers are expected to spend almost all of their time with students. There are very few opportunities for the adults who operate the schools to spend nearly enough time with each other to reflect, dialogue, make collective decisions, and seek changes that will address their concerns. An important organizational arrangement that is discussed later in this chapter is the reading-improvement committee. The formation and careful work of this kind of committee is perhaps the best strategy for overcoming obstacles and dealing with conflicts that accompany change.

For many schools these ideas for selecting strategies to overcome specific obstacles and conflicts are in and of themselves significant changes. But in more and more schools these ideas are enabling teachers to forge new ways to overcome obstacles and deal with the conflicts that inevitably accompany change. Of course, all conflicts can never be identified and resolved by these suggestions. The best that can be done is to maintain the integrity of the adults who comprise "the system." Everyone's feelings and perceptions matter, and professional growth is best assured through mutual planning on the part of teachers and principals.

Some Final Words on Change and Conflict

In this chapter the major components of change were discussed. The approach taken was to present a detailed picture of how and why it is necessary to select change strategies to overcome specific obstacles that stand in the way of making improvements. The truth is that conflict and change go hand in hand because change means altering roles, relationships, and working conditions. Failure to come to grips with obstacles to change is perhaps the major barrier to improving school reading/writing instruction. The bottom line is that strategies that are carefully selected to overcome specific obstacles are the key to successful change. The following case study of how one school improvement effort proceeded will illustrate this point repeatedly.

Martha and Lorna Adopt Two Professors

The parochial school where Martha taught fourth grade was in trouble. The morale was low, teacher turnover was high, test scores had dropped, and more parents were transferring their children to the public school. Martha came to our offices one day with a proposition. In a previous diagnostic reading class Martha had read about an idea for school improvement that called for a school to "adopt" a professor who would become part of the school "family." The adopted specialist could provide help and support in exchange for a place to do research. Martha had remembered this and so her pitch was simple. "We have problems where I teach. Would you and Dr. Smith (another professor) consider being adopted?" Although we were initially a bit reluctant we were also curious. So we agreed to look into the idea.

The initial step was a meeting with Martha, the school principal, and the parish priest to explore the possibility. At the meeting we discussed the school's problems and strengths. It was agreed that in two weeks we would attend a faculty meeting to consider the idea of having the staff adopt two professors.

This adoption plan of monthly meetings lasted four years, and although Martha has another job at a higher-paying school, Dr. Smith and I still have a good relationship with the staff. Lorna, the principal is still at the school, and although there is a 50 percent turnover in the staff, the teachers meet monthly and there is evidence of school improvement in reading and language arts. In place of only basal readers, teachers use literature and writing as the basis for reading instruction. Instead of spelling workbooks, weekly word lists are generated from content area units and the students' writing. There is sustained silent reading and cross-grade shared reading, and monthly staff meetings are marked by enthusiastic sharing of ideas and open discussions of successes and problems. It was not like this when the adoption plan was in the early stages.

Trust Takes Time

As experienced teacher educators, we were not surprised to find that our initial meetings with the classroom teachers were marked by a definite tension. After all, we were "strangers." One reason for this is that in the presence of outside "experts" there is a tendency for teachers not to share ideas or express opinions for fear of criticism. Another, and perhaps more basic, reason for this tension is that teachers tend to ask specific questions that pertain to specific situations and specific students. And as professors we are guilty of giving general answers that may not be perceived immediately as being helpful (Lanier, 1983). The plain fact is that classroom teachers and professors have a different orientation to school and learning and teaching. In addition, teachers tend to be very private about what they do in their classrooms. So it was not until after we had met over a three-month period that teachers felt safe to share and ask questions. The first sign of real progress toward common issues came when teachers agreed that the school office needed to be relocated and they needed a lounge-work space area. The principal was supportive of these concerns and a parent-architect-contractor committee was formed.

More progress toward school improvement in reading and writing came when one teacher approached us after our fifth monthly meeting and quietly and privately shared her excitement about her increased use of library books (and less use of the basal reader) in language arts. At the next meeting, she shared her story of new student interest and enthusiasm for reading with the other teachers and the principal. Another teacher and the principal verified her experience and this seemed to mark the beginning of a more open climate of exchange and of our being "adopted."

As the first year ended two other ideas were discussed and implemented by the teachers before school ended in June 1988. The first idea came from Judy, the sixth-grade teacher. She had shared her success with having a sustained silent reading time using paperback books. After discussing Judy's success with motivating students to read, the staff arranged a cross-age/grade paired reading time so that fifth graders read with first, sixth with second, seventh with third, and eighth with fourth graders. The second idea was to teach spelling and vocabulary from a student-centered viewpoint. In place of the weekly workbook list, teachers chose words from content area material they were studying and words that students were having trouble with and which they wanted to learn to write. From March to the end of the year in 1988 both ideas were tried by all of the teachers and our monthly meetings were spent sharing successes, problems, and working together to iron out hitches. The faculty was unanimous in their support for continuing the reading and spelling changes. They also supported continuing our monthly meetings!

The adoption has taught all of us a number of things:

1. Initial contacts created visible tensions and it took at least five months of meetings before open exchange of ideas was possible.
2. Initial ideas for changes always came from the staff. They never came from the professors. Teaching ideas that led to changes had already been tried by a teacher in isolation and the meetings became a place to disclose or suggest a possible improvement.
3. The principal's involvement, active support, and listening kept the monthly meetings going. Her support was crucial to the success of the teacher-professor meetings.
4. The monthly meetings became an important forum for teachers to share their power for planning instruction with each other and the principal.
5. Changes were implemented because there was a balance of input from within and from outside the school. This balance was sustained long enough for teachers to try out ideas and receive support, hints for success, and recognition.

6. The professors' most effective tasks were to be good listeners and support teachers' ideas with research. Time and again teachers and the principal said they felt more confident about what they were doing because we had "backed them up" at the meetings.

Perhaps this teacher's comment helps explain why Martha's adoption idea has worked. "We talk, we get excited, and I go back to my kids feeling I have to implement what we talked about because I'll have to report what happened at the next month's meeting." The anticipation of another meeting of true sharing is evidence that the initial pothole of a lack of trust had been replaced by a show-and-tell attitude. The total staff of ten teachers, the principal, and the two professors acted like a team that gathers after a game to talk, laugh, and argue about both the good plays as well as the errors.

Summary

Changing the status quo in schools creates conflicts that are best handled by acknowledging them and selecting activities to overcome them. Underlying the change process are important ideas, such as acknowledging adult stages of change and the need to collaborate to overcome the isolation that teachers experience. Strategies for overcoming typical obstacles were reviewed and a case study of how a teacher and a principal adopted two professors to support school changes was described.

Collaboration is a basic concept that deserves a detailed discussion, and the next chapter looks at how small teams of teachers collaborate to implement changes.

References

Andrews, T. E., Houston, W. R., and Bryant, B. L. (1981). *Adult learners.* Washington, D.C.: Association of Teacher Educators.

Becoming a nation of readers: The report of the commission on reading. (1985). Washington, D.C.: National Institute of Education.

Carnine, D. (1988). How to overcome barriers to student achievement. In S. J. Samuels and P. D. Pearson (Eds.), *Changing school reading programs.* Newark, Del.: International Reading Association, 59–91.

Erickson, L. (December 1981). I'd like to but I don't think I can. *Educational Leadership, 39,* 194–195.

Erickson, L. (Spring 1982). Reading inservice? Yes. Improved instruction? Maybe. *Michigan Reading Journal, 15,* 60–62.

Erickson, L. (September 1987). Staff development: Five ways to keep things in focus. *The Executive Educator, 9,* 24.

Fraatz, J. (1987). *The politics of reading.* New York: Teachers College Press.

Lanier, J. E. (1983). Tensions in teaching teachers the skills of pedagogy. In Griffin, Gary A. (Ed.) *Staff development.* Eighty-second yearbook of the national society for the study of education. Chicago: University of Chicago Press.

Leithwood, K. A., (Ed.). (1986). *Planned educational change. A manual of curriculum review, development, and implementation (CRDI) concepts and procedures.* Toronto: The Ontario Institute for Studies in Education.

Lieberman, A., and Miller, L. (1984). School improvement: Themes and variations. *Teachers College Record, 86,* 4–19.

Shannon, P. (Winter 1986). Teachers' and administrators' thoughts on changes in reading instruction within a merit pay program based on test scores. *Reading Research Quarterly, 21,* 20–35.

Weik, K. W. (1976). Educational organizations as loosely-coupled systems. *Administrative Science Quarterly, 21,* 1–9.

4

Collaborate to Improve Literacy Instruction

The work of committees can be deadly serious business, especially when there is a need to forecast the future. By instinct, each of us knows that this is a responsibility not to be trusted to any single person; we have to do it together.*

This chapter describes how teams of teachers collaborate to implement changes in reading and writing instruction. The intent is to show how teams are formed, how they work, what guidelines they follow, and what a typical team agenda looks like. Some of the material in this chapter is based on case studies (Erickson, 1990), while other information comes from the growing body of knowledge about how collaboration works in schools.

A basic point of beginning in this chapter is that, although reports of teacher to teacher collaboration are on the increase, teaching is basically a private and lonely enterprise. Although relations with students are daily and direct, relations with fellow teachers are remote, oblique, and defensively protective, and a climate for privacy governs peer interactions in a school (Lieberman and Miller, 1984). Because teachers protect them-

*Lewis Thomas, 1979. *The Medusa and the Snail*, p. 117.

selves and maintain their security by being very private about how they teach, there is a natural and self-imposed resistance to teaming with peers. We need to keep in mind that collaboration itself is a huge change for experienced teachers who have functioned independently.

Despite these realities, teams do exist. At the ConVal District in New Hampshire, improvement teams of teachers and administrators have created an atmosphere of cooperation, collaboration, and trust rich in risk taking and idea sharing. Innovation in teaching reading and writing is highly valued and teachers are encouraged to initiate improvements and curricular adaptations (Robbins, 1990). In Illinois, from suburban Chicago to southern towns such as Chester and Jonesboro, schools have improvement teams headed by teachers that negotiate and implement changes in literacy programs (Erickson, 1990). What follows is a detailed look at teacher-led improvement teams.

Earlier, in chapter one of this book, I discussed how teacher-change-agents emerged from their classrooms to work "in the middle" with teachers, principals, consultants, parents, and others to effect change. Working in this middle level entails committee work that is different from working alone in the classroom. It requires new skills. This chapter describes how the skills of negotiation, collaboration, and shared decision making are applied to changing literacy instruction.

Why Form Improvement Teams?

Perhaps the main reason collaboration is difficult is that reducing isolation also reduces one's autonomy—making one more susceptible to the influence of others. For some teachers, this reduction in autonomy may be too threatening. On the other hand, "experiencing rewarding contact with their colleagues, teachers may come to rely less on the classroom setting as the source of all their professional rewards" (Fraatz, 1987, p. 199). This new source of reward and influence can help teachers feel freer to make changes and is perhaps the chief benefit of collaboration.

However, the fact remains that most reading improvements occur teacher by teacher rather than school by school (Valencia and Killion, 1988). The overall reason for this is that, in addition to working in isolation, there is much in the professional life of teachers that fosters a go-it-alone existence. They attend college classes as individuals, and they go back to implement new ideas in their classrooms as individuals. In addition, most of the published information on reading improvement is usually aimed at individual teachers who read how to implement strategies in their own classrooms. And I agree with Fullan (1985) and Leithwood (1986) that schools often lack the arrangements to guide, protect, and support schoolwide efforts long enough for changes to take hold. For the most part schools are organized and managed to run a child-learning arrangement that keeps teachers away from each other and with students most of the time. However, a close look at schools today reveals that more and more instances of teaming are observable. The opportunities for teachers to talk, reflect, make collective decisions, and collaborate to improve reading and writing instruction are on the increase, and here is how they were started.

How Are Teams Started?

Case studies of the initiating process indicate that the birth of an improvement team is somewhat unique to each individual school. There is no one way or "right" method for starting teams. Whether a team was started by a principal or several teachers is not crucial. What is crucial, however, is that once the team was started, its effectiveness and success depended on the extent to which teachers gained ownership over the team's activities. This raises questions about principals. What is their role? My observation is that perhaps the most effective principals' role in regard to improvement teams was stated by one principal at a conference in Chicago in 1990. I was leading a principal's workshop at a national meeting on how to negotiate curriculum changes. During the discussion he described how amazed he was at the changes being made by several veteran teachers. He said that, although they had started working together to implement a mandated drug awareness program, they had now moved on to integrating science, social studies, and language arts activities. He described them this way: "It's as if they had worked alone for years on one side of the river, but now they had crossed it and were on the other side working as a team. And I couldn't have forced them to cross over. But now my job is to recognize where they are, and to support them and feed them, and help them keep growing." The principal's power to sustain or kill a team is very real. If a principal trusts the teachers to team together with competence there is a good chance for effective collaboration. However, if a principal dislikes teaming or acts threatened and angry when two or more teachers get together, the negative psychological power that is generated can stifle collaboration. Simply stated, a principal sets a tone that can make or break the teachers' efforts to join together.

However, in schools where collaboration and teaming worked, the teachers had called the shots, and their efforts were supported by a principal. They often started like this:

1. Someone believed a team approach to reading improvement was worth doing and initiated dialogue with key people in the school, community, or local teacher training center. This dialogue ranged from a series of very informal conversations in the car going home after school to a more formal agenda item at a regular faculty or staff meeting. Who initiated the dialogue? Case studies reveal that it really is not so important. What is important is that at least two people met and began talking about working together. Early teaming efforts featured an authentic attempt by someone who was respected enough to influence others to begin talking and listening.

2. This initial dialogue was soon followed by some data collection. For example, a questionnaire might be distributed, or small group interviews might be conducted, or reactions to a presentation might be shared. Early activities involved a meeting either after school or during a time when school is dismissed early. In each case data on possible reading- and writing-improvement topics were collected, shared, and discussed. Of utmost importance was that the teachers prioritized their own data, and they selected reading- and writing-reform topics that they wanted to pursue in a collective fashion.

3. Following these initial meetings, individuals voluntarily joined together with either a partner or a larger team and began initiating improvement activities based on the data they had collected from their colleagues.

4. Teams selected leaders, developed their own agendas and role assignments, and arranged a calendar of meeting dates. In most cases these meetings were held during school hours when students are dismissed, although some teams were motivated to meet more often after school.

It is clear that in these case studies reading/writing-improvement activities did not happen simply because they were sanctioned by administrators and mandated in a top-down fashion. In each school teachers and principals were convinced that proposed changes made sense in their particular situation. Top-down mandates from those in power do not guarantee improvements (Corrigan and Howey, 1980; Dodd and Rosenbaum, 1986; Levine, 1985). Instead, teachers worked together and implemented improvements because they participated actively in deciding the improvement topics as well as the learning conditions.

Who Is On an Improvement Team?

The literature on successful school improvement clearly indicates that the ability of teachers to change is closely related to changes in the school power structure. When teachers work alone their rewards and incentives are focused around what they do in their own classrooms. When teams are created the source of rewards and incentives tends to move away from the classroom, and teachers tend to become influenced by other teachers, consultants, and even parents. The broader influences that come from true collaboration have the effect of freeing teachers to implement changes (Andrews, et al., 1981; Bertani, Tafel, Proctor, Vydra, 1987; Hutson, 1981; Reigel, 1987). The literature on successful change clearly indicates that when teams of consultants, teachers, administrators, and parents collaborate, they are able to: (1) influence decision making; (2) organize and obtain resources; (3) obtain school and community support; (4) use authority effectively; and (5) protect improvement efforts from attacks by internal and external interest groups. In addition, because team members represent different levels of the school hierarchy, they are better equipped to overcome the teacher-child learning orientation and to use adult learning principles to guide training sessions.

Based on observations and interviews of successful teams, innovation is possible because the top-down, bottom-up, internal and external forces that control change are balanced. In order to forge this balance the membership of a team needs to be diversified. Some of the most successful early collaboration case studies (Lambour, Rostetter, Sapir, Taha, 1980) indicate that it is important to:

1. Include members from the top, bottom, inside, and outside the school.
2. Find a structure to fit the school. In small schools (less than 15 staff) one team is possible. In larger schools it works to have two or more teams such as a primary (K–3) and an intermediate (4–6). In junior and senior high schools, teams can be arranged by departments and or grades. A general rule is to keep teams close to a dozen members or less.
3. Give members released time and/or financial compensation to participate. Some teams have a budget for materials and hiring consultant help.
4. Train team members in change agentry and adult learning.
5. Release a teacher who could coordinate the team and work up to half-time on the team's behalf.

6. Let the teams determine their own agenda rather than imposing an agenda upon the members.
7. Provide time and training for the teams to self-renew, recruit new members, acquire new skills, and plan for the future.

How Does a Team Collaborate?

Successful teams report that, because the members represent a variety of diverse viewpoints, collaborating requires special group process skills to avoid shouting matches. Another reason teams need help is that, as educators, we are most often trained to lead children. Managing a classroom can be quite different from negotiating and compromising with other adults in order to agree on reading/writing improvement goals and activities. Some appropriate activities used early in the life of committees enable members to negotiate and collaborate on literacy-improvement initiatives. Sample activities include (Erickson, 1981; Erickson, 1983):

1. At early meetings, team members discussed their ideas and attitudes on reading/writing improvements. Giving adults a chance to share their values, opinions, past experiences, and concerns early in the life of the team helps build trust and "unfreeze" communications. An example of a good activity is to have members write answers to the following question: What individual and institutional factors inhibit reading/writing improvements in schools? After writing alone, small groups share responses, and one member reports group responses to the entire team. Often this "list" of ideas is used to begin the planning process.

2. Teams continue to meet monthly (or more often) and their work is never completed because change is a developmental process that requires continual effort. Unforeseen developments and unexpected events occur along the way, and teams need to rethink, reformat, and adjust reading initiatives. The continued contact between administrators, teachers, and parents minimizes conflicts and promotes timely corrective action.

3. The teams study and discuss materials on adult learning and change, and often someone helps the group plan steps for long-range change. This training is often carried out by a local educator, although a carefully selected "outsider" can be effective. Examples of excellent resources include Samuels's and Pearson's *Changing School Reading Programs* (IRA, 1988) and Alvermann et al. *Research Within Reach: Secondary School Reading* (IRA, 1987). Excellent articles also can be found in the *Journal of Staff Development* and *Educational Leadership*.

4. Team leadership skills are especially crucial when attempts are made to change the status quo. In many teams, effective leadership is often displayed by someone other than a high-status school official. Often an articulate and respected teacher can lead sessions. Skill in group processes and consensus decision making is more important than high status due to expertise or position.

5. Effective teams follow carefully planned agendas. Open discussion free-for-alls are controlled by time limitations, and an agenda that features some writing in each phase has helped team members communicate as they collaborate. Writing is important to collaboration because it allows three important kinds of listening to occur. First, each person perceives that everyone else has considered his or her thoughts because they were recorded for everyone to read; second, each person reads (and therefore considers) everyone else's recorded ideas; and third, as the group generates lists, members can see some evidence that they are making progress toward shared agreements on literacy improvements. For example, here is a list of shared thoughts that were developed by a team. Notice how school improvement activities are expedited because the team of teachers, department heads, and administrators collectively wrote the following guidelines for their school improvement activities: (1) The program must provide practical "teacher proved" ideas that teachers can use to meet individual student needs; (2) the program must allow teachers time to try out teaching ideas and then discuss successes and concerns; (3) teachers must have some financial incentive to implement new teaching techniques; (4) the program must use resources of staff members who are already working in the local school system; (5) techniques learned and practiced in summer workshops must be implemented during the following school year.

Agendas that feature writing are presented in detail in chapter six of this book in the section Decisive Formats. The nominal group-writing plan and the participatory ranking are especially useful agendas that feature writing.

6. Experienced teams are realistic about the length of time needed for schoolwide literacy improvements to take hold. Significant schoolwide improvements may take from three to five years to be fully implemented. A realistic long-range time frame allows a semester for a team to agree on working arrangements and gather initial data. It is not unrealistic for successful teams to spend up to one school year setting goals, planning improvement activities, and negotiating specific issues before initiating improvements. A sample time line may be:

1st Semester—Team formation, initial meetings, training in school improvement.

2nd Semester—Gather data from interviews, questionnaires, and tests; prioritize goals; plan and implement initial improvement activities.

7. Teams are excellent vehicles for overcoming barriers that threaten to stall or kill schoolwide reading/writing improvements. In a recent team meeting teachers were learning about using advance organizers to help junior high students comprehend poetry. Some teachers warned that taking time to carry out the pre- and post-reading activities would prevent them from using all of the poems and stories in the text. The team agreed and arranged sessions in which teachers and administrators agreed on deleting stories and poems. The team decision made it safe for teachers to skip some material. Providing students and teachers with more time for higher-level thinking was deemed more important than covering all of the text material.

What Does a Team Agenda Look Like?

The following plan can be used as a guide for helping teams work smoothly. Case studies of successful school teams reveal that the following agenda is useful for collaborating to implement long-range improvement initiatives (Erickson, 1983; Second Opinions, 1984).

1. *Define roles.* In order for members to act collectively they need to agree on common issues and defined goals. They do this by collecting written responses to questions such as: What reading/writing improvement issues will this team deal with? What product will it produce? Is it expected to develop policy, carry out policy? To whom does this team report? Responses to such questions are recorded and discussed at initial meetings, and the group records its final statements for everyone to use in future work.

2. *Define authority.* After the team begins to work, it is necessary to clarify its power and influence. Confusion about this can cause some members to believe that they only recommend initiatives, while others think they are preparing to lead an implementation activity. Also, when alternate actions are proposed it is necessary to check on legal and contractual restrictions concerning staff time and money. Obtaining written answers to these questions also helps: Where does this team fit into the formal structure of the school and district? What are the time, money, and staff policy limitations to consider?

3. *Get the facts.* Improvement planning requires the use of both fact and opinion. Separating the two is not easy, but one way that seems to work is to collect written information based upon the following questions: What current curriculum policies or student data are relevant to reading/ writing improvement? Is this information valid and confirmable? Does this information alter the committee's original goals? Sources of data include interviews with administrators, teachers, experts, or reports of test data, or reports of questionnaire data from students and/or the community. Charts, reports, and diagrams are useful to report data to the team.

4. *Develop policies.* In order to expedite decision making and reach agreement it is necessary to test improvement policies and future activities against written standards. For example, consider how decision making became clearer and more direct when members of a textbook selection committee shaped their deliberations around the following agreed-upon (written) guidelines: Materials must: (1) Reflect our goal that children will become strategic readers. (2) Be relevant to our students' backgrounds and experiences. (3) Feature excellence in children's literature. (4) Feature informational and content area material. (5) Allow us to combine reading and writing activities. (6) Enable us to use portfolios and teacher observation in our assessment of student progress. Statements like this can help the team members reach consensus and have a way to evaluate the effectiveness of their text-selection activities.

School leaders report that these agenda items help adults to collaborate and not be dominated by authority figures or vocal members (Erickson, 1983). Collaborating is easier when plenty of writing materials such as flip charts, markers, paper, ballots, allow people to read each other's ideas. Reading each other's written responses, as opposed to open discussion, is a way of preserving each adult's perceptions about solutions to reading-improvement issues, while at the same time linking thought processes so that team members can reach agreement. An examination of typical agendas, documents, and reports supports the notion that a team approach makes sense, because serious school business is rarely entrusted to any one individual or segment of the school community anyway. In the following section a case study illustrates how a successful team operated in one school.

Larry's WIN Idea Improves Schoolwide Writing

In the spring of 1986 at the Chester, Illinois, grade school, I led a language arts workshop class for graduate credit. Tuition was paid by a state reading improvement grant and 15 elementary and junior high teachers enrolled. During the first three sessions, while I carried the ball and led the sessions, Larry sat in the back of the room and asked a few questions. While he was wary about the workshop and had not enrolled, he appeared curious about what we might do and asked a lot of questions. During these initial sessions I presented ideas about whole language, reading as an interactive process, and how teachers are integrating reading and writing. At the fourth session I told the teachers that since this was their workshop they ought to plan how the rest of the time should be spent. They met in groups by primary and intermediate grades, and after brainstorming, everyone shared ideas as a whole group. Much of the discussion focused on improving writing instruction, and the decision was made that we would all come back next week with specific ideas about activities we could do in the rest of the workshop to improve writing throughout all of the grades.

When I returned to the school the following week I was armed with ideas and planned a sharing agenda that I expected I would have to lead. But Larry was waiting for me in the hallway with a written proposal that he wanted me to review before the meeting started. He also had completed the forms to enroll in the workshop. As I scanned his papers he explained that he had been thinking about ways to improve the school writing program for several years. And now he had worked all weekend on his idea for an all-school writing program called Writing Is Necessary (WIN). His proposal went like this: The goal of WIN is to upgrade student writing skills by organizing all the teachers in the school to accomplish the following objectives:

1. Persuade faculty and the community to increase time and effort related to student writing activities.
2. Establish a support group of teachers to plan, monitor, maintain, evaluate, and solicit financial support for WIN.
3. Provide a yearly schedule, policies, and guidelines for WIN.
4. Develop motivational rewards and incentives for student writers.

Larry's idea was that each month of the school year there would be a schoolwide writing contest. Winners' written or artistic projects would be displayed on school bulletin boards along with winners' pictures and first-place ribbons. Winners' names and pictures would appear in the paper each month and students would read winning projects to classes at the school.

I was very impressed and told him to share his idea with the teachers. He was understandably reluctant for fear of being spurned by the other teachers. I assured him I would support his plan, so he explained his idea to the teachers. They listened to his proposal, discussed some of the details, and adopted his plan as their topic for the rest of the workshop. The agenda for the rest of the nine weeks was set and my job changed from teacher to manager and facilitator. I recall that it was hard at times for me to not play professor and lecture and bombard them with more ideas. But I bit my tongue and instead played an observer-manager role. I reacted to their ideas, supplied a few ideas, answered questions, acted as a record keeper, and kept out of their way.

The teachers divided the work among three subcommittees and they spent nine three-hour sessions after school to plan every detail of a yearlong monthly writing contest. They selected monthly themes and wrote guidelines describing how students were to write or develop artistic products for each month of the school year. They described how judging would work, how awards were to be made, and how publicity would be handled. A budget for bulletin boards, awards, paper and supplies, and film for picture taking was developed. My job as the workshop leader was helping them use TNT or time-name-task charts to make sure specific people completed their tasks by specified times.

Larry's WIN idea was implemented in the fall of 1986 and is still going strong. Larry and the teachers continue to plan each year's activities. Each month students write poetry, true stories, cartoon stories, posters, fiction, etc. and their work is displayed and read, and winners' names and pictures appear in the local newspaper. The school has new display cases so that the children's products are shared with everyone else. Writing is now a high priority activity that is promoted and celebrated in the school and community. Each month students, teachers, and parents anticipate high-quality efforts from children, and it would be hard to stop the plan because writing *is* necessary at this school.

The key to the success and long life of this program is that the WIN idea came from a teacher, and was planned in detail by a significant number of volunteers who claimed ownership. In addition, after the workshop ended, a team of teachers representing different K-8-grade levels has continued to plan, monitor, manage, and make sure the WIN program is on track.

Although there was schoolwide implementation and widespread acceptance of the WIN program, you can be sure that the program was not without its critics and naysayers in the school. In my experience I have yet to see unanimous endorsement of any change in a school setting. With the WIN program there was apparently enough overt acceptance for it to get off the ground. There was also a committee that provided some organization, materials, and support details to jog the activities along.

The Power of Having a Voice

The WIN idea is a good example of how experienced teachers already have visions of what will work to improve reading and writing programs. Larry's vision for improving writing became a reality because he thought about it for some time. He took the time to write it down so that others could read it and think about it. Most important, he shared it with others. The lesson in this is very clear. Larry had found his "voice" and told his story.

Teachers naturally think about their visions for improving classroom and school. But do they write them down in a clear and detailed fashion and share them with their colleagues? Probably not as often as they should. Certainly the social reality of privacy and loneliness that permeates teaching is one reason that most teachers do not find their voice. Another reason many teachers and principals do not write is that it takes time and is hard work. In addition, there are relatively few incentives or occasions where one might find an audience.

You will recall that Larry was nervous about sharing the WIN idea. But the workshop provided an occasion for him to try and look at what happened. He articulated his vision, he was listened to, his idea was accepted, and his agenda became the agenda for the school and for the community.

The Need for Shared Agreements

WIN also worked because the idea was supported by shared agreements across many levels of the school and the community, as well as the region and state. If you recall, the initial activity was a tuition-supported, graduate-credit workshop. This required shared funding agreements between the university (who paid me to teach the workshop) and the local educational agency (who used grant money to pay the teachers' tuition). It featured agreements on the content and process of the workshop between the superintendent's office, the school principal, and the teachers, and me as the consultant. It also featured agreements between the teachers in the workshop and all of the rest of the school faculty who agreed to implement the program. Finally, there were shared agreements between the school and the community as parents and local newspapers supported and publicized the children's writing. These shared agreements created a workshop setting where teachers had the time to work together long enough to create their own detailed plans.

Summary

The approach taken in this chapter was to present a detailed picture of how and why an improvement team is an effective way to improve reading/writing instruction. This was illustrated as a team of teachers used a workshop format to overcome obstacles that stood between their current teaching and their ideals for writing instruction. While plenty of hard work over a long time is required, in order to implement and sustain improvements that work for particular schools and individuals, the satisfaction of growth toward shared "ideals" appears worth the effort.

In the next chapter an eight-step model that teams can use to plan and implement changes in literacy learning will be presented.

References

Alvermann, D. E., Moore, D. W., and Conley, M. W. (Eds., 1987). *Research within reach: secondary school reading.* Newark, Del.: International Reading Association.

Andrews, T. E., Houston, W. R., and Bryant, B. L. (1981). *Adult learners.* Washington, D.C.: Association of Teacher Educators.

Bertani, A., Tafel, L., Proctor, J., and Vydra, J. (Spring 1987). Teachers as leaders: A district plans for new roles, new directions. *Journal of Staff Development, 8,* 36–38.

Corrigan, D. C., and Howey, K. R. (1980). *The education of experienced teachers.* Unpublished manuscript from College of Education, University of Maryland, College Park, Md.

Dodd, A., and Rosenbaum, E. (January, 1986). Learning communities for curriculum and staff development. *Phi Delta Kappan, 67,* 380–384.

Erickson, L. (December 1981). I'd like to but I don't think I can. *Educational Leadership, 39,* 194–195.

Erickson, L. (October 1983). Stop shouting! Use writing to keep group decisions on target. *The Executive Educator, 5,* 34–37.

Erickson, L. (May 1990). How improvement teams facilitate school wide reading reform. *Journal of Reading, 33,* 580–585.

Fraatz, J. (1987). *The politics of reading.* New York: Teachers College Press.

Fullan, M. (1985). Change processes and strategies at the local school level. *Elementary School Journal, 85,* 391–421.

Hutson, H. M. (Winter 1981). Inservice best practices: the learnings of general education, *Journal of Research and Development in Education, 14,* 1–10.

Lambour, G., Rostetter, D., Sapir, S. G., and Taha, A. H. (1980). *A practical guide to institutionalizing educational innovations.* U.S. Department of Education, Office of Special Education, Division of Innovation and Development.

Leithwood, K. A. (1986). *Planned educational change. A manual of curriculum review, development, and implementation concepts and procedures.* Toronto: The Ontario Institute for Studies in Education.

Levine, D. U. (Fall 1985). Bringing about instructional improvement in elementary and secondary schools. *Houghton Mifflin/educators' forum,* Boston: Houghton Mifflin, 6–11.

Lieberman, A., and Miller, L. (1984). *Teachers, their world, and their work .* Alexandria, Va.: Association for Supervision and Curriculum Development.

Reigel, M. (Summer 1987). Motivation and commitment through teacher-initiated staff development. *Journal of Staff Development, 8,* 50–53.

Robbins, P. A. (March 1990). Implementing whole language: Bridging children and books. *Educational Leadership, 47,* 50–54.

Samuels, S. J., and Pearson, P. D. (1988). *Changing school reading programs: Principles and case studies.* Newark, Del.: International Reading Association.

Second Opinions (February 1984). *Executive Educator, 6,* 2.

Thomas, L. (1979). *The medusa and the snail.* New York: Viking Press.

Valencia, S. W., and Killion, J. P. (1988). Overcoming obstacles to teacher change: Direction from school-based efforts. *Journal of Staff Development, 9,* 2–8.

5

Implementing Reading and Writing Changes

All bands at that time were mostly ear bands.
Whatever you heard you'd pick a place to fit in. You
can ask anyone who was ever in there and they'll
tell you. There wasn't any [written] music.*

Growing up in Michigan's Upper Peninsula, I learned a 1950s' jitterbug dance style that we called the Escanaba eight step. After 40 years, the eight step is still a good way for two people to coordinate their efforts and move together. The issue in this chapter is similar. I am going to describe an eight-step process that I encourage teachers and principals to learn and use when they dance to the tune of school improvement.

The plan I describe here is very similar to other typical school improvement processes, but it is more closely aligned with the work of Leithwood (1986). I find his ideas for implementing planned change in schools laced with both realism and humor. For example, he humorously acknowledges how teachers often get immediate and humbling feedback when students react to new teaching ideas. And he pokes fun at school improvement efforts by citing baseball philosopher Yogi Berra, who said, "Three quarters of this game [change agentry] is half mental" (Leithwood, p. 51). And I agree. Implementing change involves a lot more than simply following eight steps. In fact if you look at this dance step as a

---

*Bill Crow, 1990. *Jazz Anecdotes,* pp. 85–86.

surefire routine you are bound to fail. I think Otto (1991) is right when he talks about the danger of adopting a programmatic routine, because once it is in place it can have a "dead-handed effect." Who wants to dance with people who follow the routines so closely that they have a dead hand?

So when you approach school improvement, try to have some sequence of activities that make good sense. Remember, dancing is fun only when you blend routines with the right amount of intuition and improvisation. The truth is that you may have to improvise—just like the early jazz musicians who had to listen, figure out the notes to play, and trust themselves to make it sound right.

Learning to Dance Appears Difficult

When I first present this eight-step plan to teachers and principals, there is often a negative reaction to the detail and tight sequencing of tasks. But who said dancing lessons should be easy? Changing teaching practices on a schoolwide basis is an ambitious and complex undertaking. It is often very difficult and frustrating work. One reason there is resistance to following any step-by-step plan is the phenomenon of "loose coupling" (Weick, 1976) that characterizes school practices. For the most part teachers work independently, and even principals practice what some call "creative insubordination." We do not do everything our superiors tell us to do, and we often do not follow policies letter for letter. Schools are therefore loosely coupled systems.

In addition to a natural looseness that thwarts dancing together, there are a host of well-documented obstacles to change that were discussed earlier, in chapter 3: (1) the lack of knowledge about better teaching strategies; (2) the human tendency to discredit new ideas; (3) the lack of shared agreements and trust among administrators, supervisors, and teachers; (4) the lack of incentives or rewards for implementing improvements; and (5) the lack of material and human resources needed to initiate, guide, and sustain implementation efforts (Carnine, 1988; Wu, 1988; Valencia and Killion, 1988).

Along with the looseness, and the barriers to change, there is the lack of organizational arrangements to guide, protect, and support schoolwide implementation efforts long enough for changes to take hold. This lack is perhaps the most formidable barrier of all (Leithwood, 1986; Fullan, 1985). The problem seems to be that most if not all of the human energy in schools is devoted to maintaining as smooth an operation as possible (Fraatz, 1987). There are relatively few opportunities for teachers, principals, and reading specialists to spend nearly enough time with each other to reflect, dialogue, make collective decisions, and work together to achieve excellence in reading in a collaborative fashion.

The eight-step process is therefore a plan that tries, as much as is possible, to deal with the looseness, the independence, and the formidable barriers that exist in schools. The steps are derived from actual instances where school leaders have attempted to codify the messy business of closing the gap between the ideal and the current state of affairs.

Dancing Requires Close Coupling

The following narrative illustrates how one school implemented some of the reading comprehension and writing recommendations described in *A Guide to Curriculum Planning in Reading* (Cook, 1986). This guide, published by the Wisconsin Department of Public Instruction, is an excellent source for teachers seeking to involve others in improving school literacy programs. In this example the teachers completed a series of tasks that helped them, as individual professionals, and the school as an organization, become better at problem solving and generating their own solutions. Their secret for success was to work together long enough to accomplish the following eight tasks:

Preplanning Tasks

1. Form an improvement team
2. Help team set priorities for change
3. Identify dimensions for change
4. Describe full implementation
5. Describe current status and stages of change
6. Assess obstacles to growth

Implementation Tasks

7. Implement change strategies
8. Monitor progress

The time line for these tasks calls for the first six to take about a semester to accomplish. The implementation and monitoring tasks take longer, and in some ways they continue and have no specific completion date. The intent of the eight-step process is that the tasks will develop into a cyclical process that teachers and principals will be able to follow by going back to task three to set new priorities and overcome new obstacles. Each of the eight steps is illustrated in the following narrative.

1. A Reading/Writing Improvement Team Is Formed

The principal and several teachers attended a local reading conference and in the car after the meeting they discussed their interest in implementing ideas from *A Guide to Curriculum Planning in Reading* (GCPR). As they talked, they agreed that, other than district staff development days, their school has no organizational arrangement for carrying out planned changes. One of the teachers mentioned that she knew of a school that established a reading improvement committee that helped steer the improvement process. Another teacher mentioned that she would like to try some new things but did not want to "go it alone." The principal said she believed that perhaps a team should be formed to set goals and monitor activities. The following week the principal and teachers met and decided to ask the other teachers if they would be interested in improving reading/writing instruction. A first meeting date was established and several teachers voluntarily attended. They discussed the school goal of developing strategic readers and looked at some of the grade-level reading and writing outcomes described in the GCPR from Wisconsin. They agreed to establish a team that included a representative teacher from each grade level (including several of the informal teacher leaders), the principal, and two parents (representing the primary and intermediate grades).

At the first meeting the team discussed the question "What does a reading/writing improvement team do?" Each member of the team wrote his or her own answers on slips of paper and all responses were posted. The team discussed each response and the group members decided they needed a long-range time line and some outside help to guide their planning. The team then spent two more meetings agreeing on what it was to do, and the eight-step plan was proposed, discussed, and tentatively adopted. One of the teachers had recently been at a workshop on school improvement, so he shared articles and handouts about planned change, including adult learning, problem solving, and group decision making. In this way the team created an organizational structure for carrying out planned change.

2. The Team Sets Priorities for Change

During the third and fourth meetings, the team reviewed the GCPR and the teachers on the team commented favorably about many of the ideas. Establishing priorities is important in order to overcome three dilemmas (Leithwood, 1986) that plague planned change.

The first problem is that some teachers are probably already implementing some of the recommendations, so that the question "What's new?" will yield quite a variety of answers depending on each teacher's current practice. The second problem is that some recommendations may conflict with current practices. For example, ideas about having children do more writing in response to literature conflicts with current daily use of workbook exercises, so that teachers claim there is no time for more writing. One solution is to replace many of the workbook pages with journal writing and structured story-writing activities. But the teachers wisely decided to hold this suggestion until later, knowing that now was not the time to debate this specific issue. The third problem is that there is a limit to how much energy and attention any one individual can devote to a variety of efforts at one time. The psychic demands of teaching, plus the need to always be with students, limits the energy and time that are necessary for planning and implementing new practices. Teachers agreed that replacing "fill in the blank" workbook pages with better writing activities makes good sense, but felt that they lacked the expertise, time, and energy to decide what to delete and what to replace.

These three dilemmas support the need to set priorities. Many shared agreements between the staff are needed just to make a single change. And if too many changes are attempted at the same time, too many obstacles will doom the chances for success. The principal was convinced that it is preferable to do a few things well than many things poorly. To make sure of this she suggested the following questions and procedures to help the team involve all of the teachers in establishing a small list of agreed-upon priorities. The team considered the following questions, and the teacher representatives agreed to interview all of the other teachers.

1. What recommendations for students and teachers in the GCPR are different from our current practices?
2. What current reading practices do we need to examine and improve?

The results of the interviews were collected and the team made a list of the highest-priority items, based upon the teachers' responses and the parents' and principals' concerns. From this list the team decided to identify no more than five goals for change. These goals represented the ideal reading/writing attitudes, behaviors, and strategies that the staff desired for themselves and students. Using these goals as targets, the team was now ready to help teachers identify the critical practices they will want to change in order to reach the five goals.

At this point in the eight-step dance the following anecdote may be in order to check our location. I want to emphasize an important point about priorities as they relate to the three dilemmas of what's new, time, and energy. In schools where teachers have successfully dealt with the issue of dropping a long-held practice to make time for a new one—such as more open writing and fewer workbook exercises—gradual change over time is the rule. At St. Mary's School in Chester, Illinois (remember Martha and Lorna and the adopted professors in chapter 3?), the teachers identified several teaching practices they wanted to change. These were identified during the first four meetings. But they met for seven months (October to April) before they committed to trying to replace reading and spelling workbooks during the next year! Even then every teacher did not implement this at the same rate. What happened is that two teachers were already doing this in the spring months. They would come to the monthly school improvement sessions and share what happened when they replaced workbooks with writing. Their enthusiasm and growing confidence, as well as positive student responses, helped other teachers gradually make the shift. In the fall more teachers joined in, and after four years, writing had replaced the workbook in reading and spelling lists were generated from stories and content material on a schoolwide basis. Dependency on workbooks became the exception, not the rule. This change was made gradually, slowly, with lots of trial and error. It was supported by monthly teacher-to-teacher discussion and support from the principal and the "adopted" reading professors.

3. Teachers Choose the Critical Dimensions for Change

Because teachers do many different types of activities with students, it will be helpful to select only those specific things that need to be altered in order for the staff to see their own growth toward implementation. For example, one goal of the primary-grade teachers is to use more open writing and less workbook fill-in-the-blank writing when students respond to narrative-text literature. In order to grow toward this ideal, the teachers look at which of these six dimensions of teaching (below) need to be altered in order to implement change. The reason for this step is that rarely do all six dimensions need to be changed. This step can save time and energy by focusing attention on the main issues related to the specific idea being implemented. If this step is overlooked the result can be needless discussion and some confusion, because there is a tendency to mix these six dimensions all together. The result of such a mix is that it is hard to tease out the crucial elements of instruction and focus on specific elements to change. This step may seem tedious and picky but experience has shown that it can help the teachers reach agreements faster and with less fear of having to make too big a leap into the "unknown."

Goals/Objectives
Because the staff is involved in the interviews, and there is a consensus about implementing selected recommendations, the teachers' goals serve as the primary common set of outcomes. The decision on goals has been made and the teachers are now ready to implement the priorities they set in step two of the eight-step dance.

Content
The primary teachers agree that they will not have to change materials. Many stories in the basal reader, as well as a good supply of children's literature, will be excellent resources for stimulating writing. The point is that they do not need to buy a new basal reading series. They want to purchase more children's literature books, but current reading materials will not have to be significantly altered to achieve their goal.

Teaching Strategies
This dimension will require some changes because the primary teachers have traditionally used the reading workbook for independent seat work. Teachers will want help and support in changing from the total work-book-based response activity to a more open writing format. This issue was addressed back in step two in the example from St. Mary's school that described how teachers continued to meet together and gradually changed over a four-year period.

Materials and Resources
This dimension will also require some changes because the teachers will want help in deciding which workbook activities to keep and which ones to delete. They will seek help in how to teach young students to keep journals and other writing formats.

Assessment Procedures
These will also require some new teacher thinking, especially about how to respond to invented spelling and to the range of young children's writing abilities. This dimension of teaching is also related to parents' reactions to children's early writing. The implication is that teachers need to be prepared to explain the features of early writing to the parents.

Classroom Management
This dimension also requires some adjustment on the part of some teachers. Because a few teachers said, "But they can't write yet!" it was decided to either have teachers visit a classroom where young children

are writing or have a teacher who is using more writing explain what goes on in her classroom.

4. The Teachers Develop a Description of Full Implementation

In order to achieve the ideal goals and outcomes they have set for students and themselves, the teachers selected one of the six dimensions from step three. In their description of full implementation, they wrote that primary-grade students will respond to narrative literature by writing their reactions, their own stories, and other comments in journals. The teachers selected the classroom management dimension and described the time, space, and routines that will exist when students are writing on their own in journals. In the same manner the teachers described what full implementation would be for the remaining five dimensions. Owing to differences in teachers, the descriptions will include different actions, behaviors, and choices. The teachers are assured that, while they are all adopting some fundamental practices that will help students be better writers, each of the descriptions of full implementation denotes something that can be accomplished in a variety of ways.

The task of describing full implementation allows the staff to see that change can involve a one for all (the student goal), all for one (the content, materials, resources, assessment procedures), and everyone for herself/himself (teaching strategies, classroom management) plan. This becomes increasingly clear when task five is carried out.

5. Teachers Describe Current Status and Stages of Growth

Changes do not occur in a vacuum. All of the teachers are already teaching children to write in a number of ways. Some of these existing practices will be radically different from those described in the full implementation task; others may be very close. So the teachers select two of the dimensions for change (materials, resources, and classroom management) and ask, "What types of independent seat work are we presently using that are totally different from our description of full implementation?"

Then they describe some stages of growth from the current practice to full implementation for each of the remaining four dimensions. In this way they can see that they are at different points in the growth process. Those who are closest to full implementation may feel motivated. They can see they do not have far to go and they can serve as models for others. Those who are farther away will have some benchmarks to see that they are making progress. The stages of growth can be motivating because, as adult learners, teachers often prefer to figure out their own ways to try out new ideas and learn new skills. And, in discussions about moving toward full implementation, teachers will be concerned about specific obstacles that threaten their growth.

6. The Team Assesses Obstacles to Growth

There is no best way to remove all of the real and imagined barriers to implementation. And it will be counterproductive to try to identify all of them. One approach is to simply make a decision. Choose a barrier or obstacle and discuss strategies for resolving the problem. Another approach is to identify the problems that are particular to a specific goal for change. For example, if the goal of change is to replace some of the reading workbook exercises with writing, a common obstacle for teachers is the potential negative reaction of parents, and some teachers, to invented or immature spelling. However, several other teachers who have already overcome this obstacle share their experiences. They share the written materials they developed for parents that explained the stages of spelling development, and showed how children's spelling gradually moves closer and closer toward the "correct" conventions. They told how they used these materials at conferences and sent examples home.

The purpose of assessing obstacles to growth is to keep track of what may be preventing movement toward full implementation. A good question to use is "What must be done to remove or lessen the obstacle?" The answer will often yield a specific solution as to the level of action (at the individual, school, or district level) and the specific activity (individual support and training, team coaching, schoolwide staff development, or systemwide professional development). For example, teachers may claim that a change will run counter to the principal's orientation. A good strategy for this obstacle is better communication via an open discussion between the teacher(s) and principal about the change. The reason this works to reduce barriers is that principals "take their cues from teachers . . . consenting to and often supporting the teacher's plans" (Fraatz, 1987, p. 115).

7. Teachers Implement Change Strategies

At this point the team decides to develop task-name-time (TNT) documents that specify *tasks, names* of people who are responsible for each task, and *times* for task tryouts. For example, here is a portion of a sample TNT document that was developed.

Major Implementation Task: Replace least effective reading workbook activities with journal writing and other student centered reading/writing activities.

Sub Task	Person(s) Responsible	Date/Time
a. Staff Development on alternatives to reading workbooks	Sue (Principal)	January 10 (Early dismissal)
b. Workshops to develop new materials to use in place of workbooks	Mary, Janet, Tom	January 17 February 3
c. Try out new materials	Primary teachers	February to June

In addition to the TNT charting, the team produced a memo describing their proposed tryout plan during February to June. The memo describes the activities that they hope will enable teachers to move from the awareness/interest stage, through the mental tryout and trial stage, to the adoption and integration phase of replacing ineffective workbook activities with effective reading/writing ideas. The memo illustrates how they plan to match stages of teacher concerns with specific learning goals and activities. Box 5-1 shows the memo from the team that describes how they plan to "dance." In essence, this document describes the implementation plan and is an extension of step seven of the eight-step process.

This example of an implementation plan (step seven of the "dance") reveals two levels of change. At the individual teacher level, the memo described activities that match the concerns adults have when they encounter the personal barriers that thwart change. And at the school and grade level, the memo described how the reading-improvement team would function, and how peer-coaching activities would be used to overcome the host of organizational barriers that thwart planned change.

8. The Team Monitors Progress

For this task the reading improvement team uses step five (Describe current status and stages of growth) to determine what progress is being made. This task will involve taking a close look at strategies and conflicts, and growth in February, March, and April. Monitoring activities include reports from team members and teachers on what is working, what problems have arisen, and what strategies have been most and least successful. Children's writing samples and changes in the use of the reading workbook are used as evidence of growth. The team anticipates

BOX 5-1

Memo

To: Teachers
From: Reading Improvement Team
Re: Our "Dancing" Plan for Replacing Ineffective Workbook Exercises

Awareness/Interest Stage [January]

Need/goal: In the *awareness* portion of the dance we may not be ready to move. We'll act stiff, be passive, reveal few opinions, and not ask questions about workbook activities. We need brief, positive, and attention-getting activities that will reveal our individual and collective concerns about the positive and negative features of workbook activities. As interest grows we'll voice concerns, ask questions, respond realistically, and discuss ideas. If we meet weekly we may go through this stage in about a month. If we only meet monthly this stage may take two or three sessions.

Awareness activities. We will:

1. Write down a few comments and concerns about workbook activities using the following prompt: In five minutes or less list some good and bad examples of workbook activities you have encountered while teaching reading/writing.
2. Discuss these written statements and make a list of good and bad uses of workbooks.
3. Read excerpts from a reprint or short article that addresses some of our concerns about workbook use.
4. Discuss some possible changes that may address our concerns. We will keep this portion of the activity rather brief (no more than 20 to 30 minutes).
5. Follow up this awareness activity by making sure everyone gets a copy of the reprint, a list of the concerns that were discussed and, if possible, some of the changes that were proposed.

Interest activities. We will:

1. Link our concerns to examples of practices that improve or replace ineffective workbook exercises. We will have multiple copies of articles and other printed examples of new reading/writing ideas for interested teachers.
2. Schedule a series of short meetings with interested teachers to share and present new and alternate workbook practices.

Mental Tryout and Trial Stage [January–February]

Need/goal: At this point some of us will say, "It won't work in my class," or "I'd like to try it," or "Has this worked any other place?" Others may even

Continued

BOX 5-1   *Continued*

go ahead and attempt some new practices on a small scale or temporary basis. We can best meet these concerns with testimonials and case studies that testify to the worth and success of new reading/writing practices. The goal at this point is to address our specific concerns with practical and specific examples, as well as training activities for those who are ready to do it! While the duration of this stage is somewhat dependent upon how often we meet, experience indicates that the mental tryout stage comes rather quickly on the heels of successful interest/awareness activities. However, the trial stage is much longer. While some of us may be eager to begin, most of us approach tryouts cautiously, quietly, and on our own. These individual differences mean that the trial period will vary from person to person. We plan to allow several months for us to get a feel for replacing workbook exercises with new reading/writing activities.

Mental tryout activities. We will:
1. Read written case studies of what other teachers have done to replace ineffective workbook exercises.
2. Watch a video or recorded interview that explains a successful reading/ writing activity.
3. Listen to a satisfied and successful teacher who has implemented changes in workbook activities.
4. Listen to a panel of teachers explain their experiences and respond to our questions about changing their use of workbooks.
5. Visit a school and observe a teacher who has already adopted new reading/writing activities to replace ineffective workbook practices.

Trial activities. We will:
1. Have an informal meeting (serve refreshments) with teachers who want to go ahead, as well as those who have gone ahead on their own. At this meeting we hope to share experiences openly and give plenty of support and recognition.
2. Use interviews and questionnaires to document problems and barriers that were encountered during early trials. We will discuss ways to overcome these barriers (more time, more modeling, easier/shorter lessons and materials, more guided practice, etc.).
3. Deliver specific materials and equipment to individual teachers so that they can implement practices on their own at their own pace.
4. Arrange specific dates, times, locations, and write statements of what we envision as future use of workbook materials and effective reading/ writing activities.
5. Arrange sessions in which a classroom teacher demonstrates reading and writing techniques in a clear and realistic manner.
6. Use a commitment sign-up sheet. Signers agree to use new reading/ writing workbook practices 20 or more times over a specified period.

BOX 5-1 *Continued*

7. Help each teacher find another teacher to dance with. It is very useful to coach each other as we implement new reading/writing practices.

Adoption/Integration/Continuation Stage [February–May]

Need/goal: As we begin adapting our teaching and integrating new practices into our daily routines, we need support from coaching techniques that provide feedback and recognition. At this point the goal is to make our own decisions based on feedback from each other. We will also need recognition from peers and others from both inside and outside the school to sustain the implementation process. The following support activities are necessary, because this stage brings frustration, conflict, and controversy and is the longest and most complex portion of the change process. For example, the length of time needed to replace ineffective workbook exercises with reading/writing activities is best estimated in terms of semesters and school years rather than months.

Adoption/integration activities. We will:

1. Create peer coaching arrangements (Showers, 1985) with pairs of teachers who both act as "coaches" and "players." We will meet together, watch each other teach, and give each other feedback. We will support each other as we go through the trials and errors of learning to use new reading/writing activities.
2. Arrange sessions for sharing that emphasize the need to adapt and modify, and deemphasize the need for immediate and rigid applications. Effective peer evaluation is informal, nonjudgmental, and ongoing. All evaluation decisions will be based on criteria we develop and refine during the trial and training stages.
3. Use consensus decision-making activities rather than authority/majority voting methods. Consensus agendas feature small-group discussions, plenty of writing and balloting, and list making. Meetings and decisions will not be dominated by school officials.
4. Publicize what we are doing by having sharing sessions with other schools, with the board of education, and with the media. Videos and other media may be used to make presentations to disseminate the use of the new reading/writing activities.
5. Collect and display samples of student work, and results of successful activities will be publicized through school newsletters, and bulletins to parents.
6. Keep portfolios that attest to our efforts to use new reading and writing ideas that replace ineffective workbook exercises. We will keep journals and records that we review as a team. Here is a sample journal format:

Continued

BOX 5-1   *Continued*

Individual Teacher Journal

Name ————————————————————— Date of Entry —————————

Describe how you are implementing changes in your classroom regarding

——

——

1.   Information/knowledge acquired:

2.   Teaching skills developed/refined:

3.   Attitudes altered/improved:

4.   Professional expertise: How are the ideas, skills, and attitudes affecting your role as a professional teacher?

Signature ————————————————————————————————————

Verification by Reading Improvement Team

Date ——————————————————————————————————————

Comments:

Verified by ——————————————————————————————————

some new problems and conflicts, so they meet monthly to adjust time lines, resolve conflicts about which specific workbook materials to alter, and keep communication open. In response to some parent concerns about invented spelling, Sue and two primary grade teachers presented a parent workshop on writing in March. One outcome of this workshop was an April home-school newspaper. It featured children's writing as well as explanations of the reading and writing connections.

In late May the reading improvement team prepared a brief three-page report for the school that discussed progress, problems, and future directions. The report recommended that the work of the reading-improvement team and the staff implementation plan continue in the fall when school resumed.

The Dance Continues

Although the teachers anticipated that new goals, as well as obstacles and conflicts, would arise, they knew that they were better prepared to change, grow, and deal with conflict. As school closed the principal began the planning process to conduct a one-week workshop during the summer. She hoped to implement more curriculum changes with interested teachers. She planned to ask three teachers who had been involved with the eight-step process during the previous year to be the summer workshop staff.

Summary

A detailed eight-step plan was described that teachers and principals can use to dance to the tune of school improvement. The steps allow teachers to have the opportunity to pay careful attention to the gaps between what they image as ideal and the current status. The sequence of activities described in this chapter was as follows:

Preplanning Tasks [August-January]

1. Forming an improvement team [August–September]
2. Help team set priorities for change [September–October]
3. Identify dimensions for change [October–November]
4. Describe full implementation [November–December]
5. Describe current status and stages of change [November–December]
6. Assess obstacles to growth [November–December]

Implementation Tasks [January to June]

7. Implement change strategies
   - Write Time-Name-Task Charts [January]
   - Describe Stages and Change Activities in Memo
     - •• Awareness/Interest [January]
     - •• Mental Tryout and Trials [January–February]
     - •• Adoption/Integration/Continuation [February–May]
8. Monitor progress [February–May]

The steps provide some way to plan and monitor activities that will enable the principal, the improvement committee, and the teachers to deal with the never-ending concerns that plague school improvement. Of course, as with any dance, the eight steps in this chapter are only a basic routine that will require fine-tuning as well as a good deal of improvisation in order to be fully effective. In the next chapter, 17 adult learning formats will be presented. These formats are intended to be used with the eight-step routine you have just read about. I think you will see how they go together to facilitate school improvements in literacy learning.

References

Carnine, D. (1988). How to overcome barriers to student achievement. In S. J. Samuels and P. D. Pearson (Eds.), *Changing school reading programs*, Newark, Del.: International Reading Association, 59–91.

Cook, D. M. (1986). *A guide to curriculum planning in reading.* Madison: Wisconsin Department of Public Instruction. Bulletin No. 6305.

Crow, B. (1990). *Jazz anecdotes.* New York: Oxford University Press.

Fraatz, J. M. (1987). *The politics of reading.* New York: Teachers College Press.

Fullan, M. (1985). Change processes and strategies at the local school level. *Elementary School Journal, 85*, 391–421.

Leithwood, K. A. (1986). *Planned educational change. A manual of curriculum review, development, and implementation concepts and procedures.* Toronto: The Ontario Institute for Studies in Education.

Otto, W. (1991). [Reply in letters column, p. 45]. *Journal of Reading. 35*, 44–45.

Showers, B. (April 1985). Teachers coaching teachers. *Educational Leadership, 42*, 43–48.

Valencia, S. W., and Killion, J. P. (1988). Overcoming obstacles to teacher change: Direction from school-based efforts. *Journal of Staff Development, 9*, 2–8.

Weick, K. W. (1976). Educational organizations as loosely-coupled systems. *Administrative Science Quarterly, 21*, 1–9.

Wu, P. C. (1988). Why is change difficult? Lessons for staff development. *Journal of Staff Development, 9*, 10–14.

6

Implementing Change Through Adult Learning Formats

Most schools include neither time, structural arrangements, cultural norms, nor language to promote team learning, and most staff development programs only support the learning of individuals. *

I like to think of the information in this chapter as the muscle that drives the eight-step process described in the last chapter. And while many of the formats in this chapter can be used at different places in that dance, they are intended to extend step seven, implementing change processes. And as you try to piece this together with the information in chapters 5 and 6, I hope you will agree with me that we are just beginning to recognize that teachers working together is legitimate work.

Our legacy has been to think that teachers are working only when they are supervising children. Did you ever think about the use of the term *released time*? Traditionally teachers are "released" only for short times to attend required meetings. The formats in this chapter are literally descriptions of what teachers may do when they are "released" from

---

*Issacson and Bamburg, 1992. *Can Schools Become Learning Organizations?*, p. 43.

their "real" work. This sort of thinking has devalued a very important kind of work—professionals working together to improve schools.

Important as it is, working together continues to be a weakness in our profession. Why, for example, have we incorporated cooperative learning for students but not for ourselves? I think it is because we are accustomed to think of learning as an individual phenomenon, not a team or collective action. It is because we organize schools and train teachers to operate alone in a room of students. For teachers, adult cooperative learning is not familiar territory. Therefore, some of the formats in this chapter will be relatively new strategies. In this chapter, I describe a variety of formats that you can use to implement change for yourself and your colleagues. Of course, we all will continue to learn individually, but a major focus in this chapter is the need for collective learning. These formats are ways that teachers and principals might reach shared decisions and implement changes that reflect a common vision. And like all learning, these formats do not come with a money-back guarantee. Think of them as strategies that have worked elsewhere—and they may work for you.

Selecting Formats

When you implement learning activities, the goal is to use formats that will have enough impact to facilitate changes in thinking and teaching. As teachers we know this is not easy work. Sometimes we use learning formats that are too passive or too general to arouse enough interest to induce a mental tryout. On the other hand, we sometimes reject new teaching strategies simply because overzealous users pushed too hard. And while we all know the bad effects of a slow-moving and boring activity, we also know that the time line for learning a new practice is often too brief, or there is not enough time to fully integrate a new practice into our daily routine.

While there is no perfect mix of watching, listening, speaking, discussing, and practicing, we do know that paying attention to learning formats is important. In this chapter some of the more potent and practical learning formats are described and briefly analyzed. My intent is to present a selection of basic formats that you can use as a menu for implementing activities and processes that result in the changes your team is pursuing. Each format is not a complete learning activity in itself. A series or combination of formats carefully put together can help you arrange highly successful learning activities for teachers.

I have grouped the formats discussed in this chapter into categories according to the following functions: introductory, informative, decisive, interactive, and productive. Introductory formats break down communication barriers, promote interest in given topics, and enable adults to relate the topic to their concerns. Informative formats present ideas and disseminate content. Decisive formats promote group consensus, successful negotiation, and decision making. Interactive formats help generate ideas, promote discussion, and help teachers sustain their interest and efforts to change. Productive formats allow teachers to make specific plans, create teaching materials, and help them implement changes in their classrooms.

If you notice, these categories imply a sequence that goes from introductory or initial learning, to productive or eventual implementation and adoption. While this sequence has some logic that may help your team select formats that have the right impact at the right time, I also know that implementation is not always smooth and logical. In other words, select as you best see fit and don't worry about using them out of sequence. Trust that your best judgment as teachers will guide your use of these implementation formats. Each format description contains statements about intent, procedures, limitations, and applications.

Introductory Formats

When we ride in an elevator with strangers it is usually very quiet. We look down or up, sometimes sideways, but usually eye contact is avoided and no one says much. A similar atmosphere exists when we find a seat at the first meeting of a committee or class. The general reluctance to talk in these situations indicates how we have learned to act as if we were all alone, when in fact we are not. The tendency for adults to keep quiet and not interact can be a detriment to learning. Fortunately there are formats that we can use to overcome elevator behavior. Perhaps the simplest is to ask people to introduce themselves, tell about their work, their family, their reason for attending, or other information they think necessary. A variation of this is to have people form pairs, introduce themselves to each other, and then have each one introduce the other to the rest of the group. Pairs can be formed by asking people to turn to someone seated next to them. A bolder plan is ask people to get up and find someone they don't know. An even bolder format is to have participants respond in writing to a stimulus question and reveal something about themselves. The idea is to go beyond the usual name, job, and family information to more personal or specific information that provokes some feelings of humor, pride, or other emotions. When this works well the elevator behavior is dropped easily, and adults are moved closer to a situation in which true dialogue and learning occur. The following formats are examples of ways to help adults overcome the natural tendency to act alone in the presence of others.

Favorite Adjectives

One example of a bolder introductory format is what I call favorite adjectives. This format is a good way to get a group of strangers talking to each other, learning each other's names, and telling each other who they are. You can do it orally or prepare a one-page handout. Here is how it works. Ask the participants to write down four adjectives that describe their favorite animal, then four more for their favorite color, and four for their favorite body of water. Finally, ask them to write down four words that would describe their feelings if they were locked all alone in an all-white room with no windows and no door. Here is how a handout for this activity might look.

FOUR ADJECTIVES

1. ANIMAL	
2. COLOR	
3. BODY OF WATER	
4. ALL-WHITE ROOM	

After everyone has had a chance to write, ask the participants to move into small groups of two or three. Direct them to share names and discuss their adjectives for about five to ten minutes. After they have had a chance to compare adjectives, debrief everyone by revealing what their responses may "mean."

Psychologists tell us that our adjectives reveal the following:

1. *Animal:*   The words indicate *who we'd like to be.*
2. *Color:*   The words indicate *how we want others to see us.*
3. *Water:*   The words reflect our *attitude toward sex.*
4. *White Room:* The words reflect our *attitude about death.*

This introductory format is best handled lightly, for it is not a serious psychoanalytic activity. It lasts about 15 to 20 minutes and works best at an initial meeting or introductory session. It helps put people at ease and can open the way for future discussion and sharing activities.

Other, more formal introductory formats require some forethought and planning and are useful in a speaker-presenter-audience situation. The following discussion of unfreezing illustrates how you can help an audience get in tune with your topic.

Unfreezing

Successful teacher meetings and reading improvement sessions often feature introductory activities that "unfreeze" the adult participants. There are three principles of adult learning (Andrews, et al., 1981) that explain why unfreezing is just as important to adult learning as stretching and warming up is to strenuous physical activity. First, we know that adults respond best to personalized instruction in which they know that the teacher recognizes their uniqueness. We also know that adults must be actively involved in controlling their own learning. Finally, unfreezing is facilitated by collecting data from the adult participants. This data lets the leader know, give recognition to, and plan for the unique needs of each participant.

Here is an example of how you can unfreeze teachers. This example is for a workshop dealing with teachers' concerns about a state-mandated reading test for elementary and secondary students.

Stage One (Five minutes). To begin the meeting hand teachers a 3x5 card and ask them to write what they hope to learn or get as a result of participating in this session. Encourage them to be truthful. Tell them *not* to put names on the cards. After they have had time to write, collect the cards.

Stage Two (Ten minutes). Explain the purpose of the session; give them a short preview of the objectives, agenda, and requirements. Presenting these in writing on newsprint, a handout, a chalkboard, or an overhead works well. Then (remember, in this example the topic is the state reading test) ask them to write a question they have about the test, or one reason they are concerned about the test. Tell them to work in groups of two or three to share and discuss their question or concern. These concerns can be either positive or negative, but tell them to give a personal response. While the teachers are discussing their concerns in small groups, the leader is reading the first cards to see if there are any misunderstandings about the purpose and goals of the session. Reading these cards will allow the leader to know something about each participant, be able to respond to individual concerns, and alter or tailor the session to these concerns.

Stage Three (Ten minutes). Stop the small-group discussions. Discuss the comments on the cards. Respond to individual comments that are especially relevant. Tell them which areas of concern will not be covered, explain why they will not be discussed, and indicate a willingness to include them at a future session. Indicate a willingness to talk with anyone who wishes to discuss a concern after the session.

This activity is one way you can begin a successful session, because teachers have been recognized, been involved, and been listened to from the beginning. This format can be used with just about any school improvement topic.

Informative Formats

An important feature of learning is exposure to information and ideas. Lectures and videos plus feedback, demonstration teaching, panel interviews, and observations that communicate information in a clear, straightforward manner are important ways to learn about teaching ideas. Each of these is discussed below.

Lecture/Videos Plus Feedback

Perhaps the most used and most misused learning format we encounter is the speaker-and-audience arrangement. When one-way, controlled output of ideas and information is called for, then a lecture or video is an efficient and simple way to present basic facts, descriptions, and examples that define terms and concepts. However, this format is limited. If your objective is to change teaching behaviors or attitudes, calling upon the most dynamic speaker or authority may begin but will not complete the process of change. This does not mean that lectures or videos should be abandoned. In many situations a speaker-and-audience format is a sound format.

One way to improve this format is to have a question-and-answer or discussion activity immediately after the presentation. Sometimes it helps to have teachers write questions on cards. These are collected and given to the speaker, who then responds to the entire audience. In a video situation it is a good idea to have an immediate feedback session. How feedback is arranged can depend upon the size of the audience, the topic, or even the seating arrangement. One idea for a large audience is to form small groups and discuss, gripe, and share concerns about the presentation. However, even when this is hampered by fixed seats, such as in an auditorium facility, encouraging individual questions from the audience may be better than not attempting anything.

The point of all this is that teachers have strong opinions, and lectures and videos should allow for feedback and reactions. If your goal is to influence teachers to consider making changes in their classroom, your strategy should be to combine lectures and videos with a feedback activity.

Demonstration Teaching

When teachers I know talk about the "real world" they are referring to their life in classrooms with the pupils. For them the real test of an idea is how it works. So an important format is to arrange a real or simulated teaching situation in a setting that includes procedures, materials, equipment, and, of course, students.

I have found that advance preparation is very helpful in making demonstration teaching a worthwhile activity. The reason is that a lot of different things occur simultaneously during a lesson. And if we do not focus our attention we can miss seeing what is important. This means that demonstrations have to focus on relatively narrow topics of concern. When I plan to do demonstration teaching I try to use the following steps to help make the activity more worthwhile:

1. One demonstration will cover one or two points. Plan a series to cover a larger number of concerns.
2. Use a skillful teacher and/or practice the demonstration lesson to refine and clarify the main points.
3. Prepare participants beforehand and tell them what to look for. A packet of materials or a detailed lesson plan can be very effective.
4. Avoid lengthy introductions, move into the demonstration quickly, and save explanations and discussion for the follow-up afterward.

This tight planning should help teachers "see" the crucial teacher and student behaviors. But increasing the clarity may also limit this format. I know that when I see others teach there is a tendency for me to reject teaching behaviors that are not compatible with my own style of pedagogy. And I have often heard teachers do this when they say, "That isn't how I do it," or "I wouldn't say it that way." To overcome this tendency try to include a follow-up activity so that observers can vent their reactions, review the purposes of the demonstration, and check out their perceptions of what they have witnessed.

Panel Interviews

In this format a panel with three to five members is interviewed by a moderator while a larger audience listens. The intent is to have an efficient way to share the ideas and opinions of a small group of experts or users with a larger audience. Usually a panel is selected on the basis of a common teaching practice. For example, a panel of teachers who are "users" or "expert practitioners" are asked questions by an interviewer who has a list of questions developed by the audience. Another example is to use this format to report the results of small-group buzz sessions to the entire group. Each buzz group sends a "reporter" to the panel to be interviewed in front of all the participants. To reduce redundancy these kinds of panels are instructed to respond only with ideas that have not already been expressed.

Observations

When we hear about a new or different teaching idea, a favorite and common format is to observe classrooms to see how they do it. While it makes sense to take a firsthand look, you should consider some of the limitations inherent in teacher watching. For example, when we are observing in a typical classroom there is little chance to communicate with the teacher or with another observer. This limits the observer's need to communicate. You can't interrupt to ask questions, predict, or seek confirmations. Some schools may have observation windows and sound systems. But in the vast majority of schools observers are cautioned to be quiet and passive. This one-way communication limits understanding and impact.

Another concern is that the unpredictability inherent in classroom teaching may interrupt the lesson. The result is that the observers do not see the teaching strategy they came to watch. And even if the teacher does get to model the strategy, a single observation may not yield much more than a general overview of what is happening. A better plan is to observe the use of a specific teaching strategy repeatedly over a period of time.

These limitations mean that observations may be overused. Observing other teachers may not have the hoped for impact that leads us to change our own behaviors. However, teacher watching is a favorite activity that can be enhanced. The trick is to:

1. Select a school and classroom that will best meet our objectives.
2. Prepare in advance to look for specific features of a lesson.
3. Plan ahead to return and act upon what we have seen.

When we return home after an observation we must plan to have a follow-up session as soon as possible, when impressions are fresh and interest is high. Individually, or at a follow-up meeting, it is helpful to get answers to the question "What vision do I now have for my teaching?" and/or "What are the implications for our school?"

Decisive Formats

As teachers we tend to have distinct and often different frames of reference. Therefore reaching consensus and making grade-level and schoolwide decisions about goals, methods, and materials is very difficult (Fullan, 1992; Miller, 1987). Two techniques, the Delphi and Nominal Group Writing-Balloting, are useful ways to get adults to communicate better and reach consensus. They have been used in organizations such as businesses and schools for over 30 years. Their value is based on the use of writing to replace open discussion, and you would probably agree with me that writing and balloting are better than shouting (Erickson, 1983). And although these formats have been around for a long time, I have found that many administrators and teachers are unfamiliar with their use. After a brief review of these older techniques I will describe how a current format, called participatory ranking (Moller and Bohning, 1992), helps teachers, parents, administrators, and students set reading program improvement goals.

The Delphi and Nominal Group Technique

With Delphi you replace open discussion with writing. Instead of meetings, send a questionnaire to teachers. Collect responses, prepare a summary of results, and circulate it again. Tell them to read what everyone else has said, consider the questions again, and respond again. They can either change or keep to their original position. Collect responses, and again give the results of this second round back to everyone. Do this a third time. Usually three cycles are enough to reach consensus. Research indicates that final answers are often more complete and satisfactory when everyone has had multiple chances to respond. If a meeting is necessary the teachers will often reach consensus quickly, without prolonged debate, because they have had a chance to "listen" to everybody else by reading and reflecting quietly and on their own. Delphi fits schools where teachers are almost always with students and where meeting regularly together to make group decisions is rare.

Unlike the Delphi, in which cases people write alone, Nominal Groups require people to write in each other's presence, discuss their ideas, and vote on them to reach consensus. You give the same questionnaire to everyone at a meeting and ask each person to respond to it in about about five to ten minutes. If the group is large, have small groups of three to four teachers discuss their responses and tabulate their results on large sheets of paper. If the group is small (ten or less) the responses and results can be indicated on a chalkboard, overhead projector, or large sheet of paper. It is important to list all responses. In cases of similar ideas it is better to list all of them rather than argue. When all ideas are listed, discuss each of them to clarify meanings and answer concerns. The next step is to ask each teacher to write his or her top preference on a slip of paper. These individual ballots are collected, tallied, and the results are posted. This final tally represents the combination of individual responses and collective balloting. The significant feature is that everyone participates by writing alone before anything is discussed. This process helps keep those who are noisier, or who can intimidate others, from dominating the teachers' efforts to reach consensus.

Both Delphi and Nominal Groups (Delbecq and Van de Ven, 1971) have been around a long time and you may have had extensive experience with their use. However, if you have not, you may wish to use the next section as a detailed example of how to combine writing and discussion to set school improvement goals in reading.

Participatory Ranking (Moller and Bohning, 1992)

This format requires a leader who knows the steps and a group of participants such as teachers, administrators, parents, and even student representatives. While this format is very close to the nominal group idea that was briefly reviewed in the previous section, the following description is more detailed. I want you to be able to see exactly how this format works to obtain consensus from a diverse group.

Preparation

To prepare for this activity you will need about one and one half to two hours. Arrange a room with tables and chairs for teams of five or six members and give them paper, pencils, a flip chart with large paper, markers, and masking tape. Try to have them sit with people they usually do not work with. This mix will help produce a broader input of ideas.

Explanation

Tell the participants that they will be assessing the strengths and weaknesses of their school reading program. Explain that in order to improve the program there must be agreement on what to focus on in order to make improvements. In addition, tell them that these agreements must be made by those who will actually implement them. Tell them the time element and the six steps: (1) Identify Strengths; (2) Identify Concerns; (3) Clarify and Discuss; (4) Vote and Tally; (5) Re-vote and Tally; and (6) Report.

> *Identify Strengths.* Ask each participant to list at least two strengths about the current reading program on a sheet of paper. Have each team share its lists and decide on which two it wants to share with the larger group. Participants write these two on the large flip chart and each team reports the strengths it listed to the whole group. Group lists are consolidated by crossing out duplicate items, and a final list of up to ten strengths is posted and left up for everyone to see throughout the entire session. By limiting each participant and group to two strengths, this step should take about 20 minutes. By beginning with strengths the session starts off on a positive note. Success with this part of the format eases tension and leads to a climate of satisfaction and progress.

> *Identify Concerns.* Ask the participants to list three concerns they have about the present reading program. Examples such as "limited time for free reading" or "lack of emphasis on critical thinking and reading" will help them generate concerns. Participants are to write silently for about five to seven minutes. Then they are to share ideas, list them on the large chart paper, and have a reporter share them with the entire group. Apparent duplicates are consolidated and one common list is made. In this phase the number of concerns is not limited, so this will take longer—perhaps 30 minutes or more. The common concerns are numbered and posted for everyone to see. This list will be a guide for discussion.

> *Clarify.* This part of the format allows anyone to speak for or against a listed concern. Concerns are addressed by number, not source, in order to separate ideas from individuals. Questions are asked, more items may be added, ideas are combined, and some items are crossed

out. A new list is made with new numbers, and the participants should have a clear idea about each one. This should take about 20 minutes.

Vote and Tally. This is a tricky part of the process so give careful directions about voting. First, have each participant, working alone, list the five most important concerns for improving the reading program. Second, tell each person to weight the most important with a 5, the second with a 4, and so on. This voting activity can be done in about 15 minutes. At this point give the participants a break, and while they are gone tally all of the weighted rankings and post the results on a large flip chart or chalkboard.

The following tally method is a valid way to determine the priorities given to the items by the entire group. Sum the weights, multiply the sum by the number of times the item was reported, and use this product as a group weighting. The highest group weightings are the highest priority items.

Item	Weighted	Sum	No. of Ranks x Sum	Priority
1	3,5,5	13	(3x13) = 39	2
2	2,4,3,5	14	(4x14) = 56	1
3	2,2	4	(2x4) = 8	3

Re-vote and Tally. This is necessary when priority rankings are very close. When items are tied or separated by only a few points, it may be hard to identify the top three or four concerns. If this is the case a re-vote and tally is conducted only on these items. Use the same procedure as the original vote to find out the top three or four items. Re-voting and tallying will take about ten minutes.

Report. On the same day, or by the next day, distribute a written report to the participants that lists both the top strengths as well as the top concerns. This listing represents the consensus of what is working well and what course of action the school will take to make improvements.

Participatory ranking is a useful format that has good potential to empower you to feel ownership for common reading program improvement goals. Your active participation in the selection of common goals is crucial and will go a long way to sustain your interest and efforts to improve your school reading program.

Interactive Formats

While the previous formats are important to adult learning, exposure to new information and consensus decision making are usually not potent enough to lead to changes in teaching behaviors. As adults we need an opportunity to chew and taste before we swallow an idea. The following formats feature discussions, debates, reactions, and simulations that serve to help us digest information. They are vital if we are seeking a level of involvement that will lead us to the point where we have the commitment to try something different. The formats that promote interaction are open-ended discussions, gripe sessions, brainstorming, and role-playing.

Open-ended Discussions

This common format usually centers on an issue or problem and assumes that some organized interaction will lead the participants to either a common decision or clearly defined disagreement. All of us have experienced a mixed bag of successful as well as miserable open-ended discussions, and I have no intention of reviewing the basics of following agendas, making motions, and keeping minutes. However, there are two formats I want to discuss briefly—the leaderless group and the case analysis. Following these formats I will review some of the features of successful open-ended discussions.

Leaderless Group

The primary goal of a leaderless discussion is to increase group involvement and group responsibility. A secondary goal is to derive a solution to a problem. Because involvement is the primary objective, the group is informed that seeking a leader is to be discouraged while seeking solutions to the problem is to be encouraged. This format requires that the group be observed by someone skilled in group processes. The observer's task is to assist the group in overcoming obstacles as they generate ideas and solutions. If necessary the observer interrupts to help the group stay on task and then withdraws as they begin again. An example of when this format is especially useful is in the early life of a new team of teachers. The goal at initial team sessions is active involvement and group responsibility rather than who is in charge or what the answers are.

Case Analysis

The typical case analysis features an open-ended discussion based on a real situation or problem that begs a solution. First, the relevant parts of the situation are presented in a scenario or narrative form. The first task is for the discussion leader to help the participants interpret the significant variables of the case. For example, in a case analysis of a teaching issue the variables may be some or all of the following: lesson goals/objectives; content; teaching strategies; materials/resources; assessment; or classroom management. If leaders know the significant variables they can provide structure and guide the participants in generating ideas and solutions. However, if discussion leaders themselves are not sure what the variables are they will have to provide less structure and let participants have more leeway. When the significant variables are identified the group can then share information, analyze alternatives, and arrive at some carefully considered decisions that fit the case under review.

Our batting average with successful open-ended discussion formats can almost always be improved. And if we look at satisfying discussions we will find several things happening. First of all, the participants had a genuine interest and stake in the problem and a need to talk about it. They also had timely and pertinent information as well as a plan of action and a timetable. They also had some accurate record keeping so that discussion outcomes were not lost, and it was easy to prepare a written report. Productive discussions were usually carried out with groups ranging from 5 to a maximum of 15 members. In other words, they were large enough to carry out the work and small enough to have considerable personal interaction. They also met in a quiet and comfortable setting where they could see and hear each other. And often the group leadership rotated as the work changed. In this way the leadership was distributed by function rather than designated by position, power, or charisma.

Finally, there is much more to an open-ended discussion than calling a group of people together. This format works when there are genuine needs and objectives, some carefully considered plans, some structured and unstructured discussion, and some timely results or some follow-up activity.

Gripe Session

I list this as an interactive format because teaching creates emotional and physical stress that we have to control. Gripe sessions are especially important for us because teaching has always been messy and shaded by ambiguity. There is a chance for disagreement on just about everything we do, from our goals on one end, to our teaching methods in the middle, to measures of achievement on the other end. In order to tolerate this ambiguity we need to have time to discuss "what's wrong with it" or "why it won't work" or "why we have to do it." We need time to acknowledge problems so that we can keep them in perspective, and so that they will not dominate. We know that if we do not talk about problems we risk falling under their influence. We then lose control and become so defensive we have little energy to be proactive or to seek alternatives.

Another reason is that for a long time, education in general, and teachers in particular, have been criticized and blamed for many things in our society. While some criticism and blame is justified, much of it is not, and so we need a time to gripe, to complain, and get things off our chests. In my work I have observed time and again, during classes on campus and in meetings and staff development sessions in schools, the need for teachers to have time to gripe and have someone listen to their complaints.

There are at least two levels of griping that we can expect to deal with using a gripe format. The first level is simply an open-ended gripe session where the goal is to complain, blame others, name-call, and vent anger and frustration. The second level involves both acknowledging problems and generating some possible solutions. In the next section I will describe a typical first-level gripe session. While this type of session may not be all that pleasant, it can have a healthy outcome. Let me give you an example.

Therapy Session

I recently was asked to meet with a group of high school teachers. The principal told me that my task was to show these content area teachers some ways to teach students who were poor readers. So I packed up a box of reprints and handouts that described how content teachers help poor readers learn from text. My plan was to give them some current and practical ideas on reading comprehension and writing strategies. However, when I met with those 15 teachers in a classroom it was quite apparent that they were not ready for those ideas. They were hostile and angry and demanded to know why they even had to teach poor readers. They were not looking for ideas to help poor readers. They were angry that they even had to be at this meeting.

Instead of going ahead with the articles and handouts I decided to sit in a circle and have a gripe session. And did they ever gripe. They complained about the state testing program, the school board, the parents, the students, and even each other. While I did my best to maintain some order, all I accomplished was to act as a sounding board. The griping continued even when the superintendent came in and sat down. And to his credit he seemed to listen and respond to some concerns.

As I recall, the session had gone on for about an hour when one of the teachers said, "This is just like a therapy session. I feel better than I did when we started." Some others acknowledged her and another teacher asked me, "Is this how other teachers feel? Have you experienced this at other schools?" I said, "Yes, some schools have regular gripe sessions to deal with teachers' concerns. They know that if they don't they will never get to the point where they will move forward to deal with student learning problems." I was telling them about how some schools have regular gripe sessions when one of the teachers said, "What do you have in your box?" I told them about my original plan and shared with them my decision to have a gripe session. I told them in general what I had in the box and said I would leave them copies. We discussed what had happened in this session, and there was general agreement that the climate in the room was now much more relaxed than an hour ago. I left them with an offer to come back to help them formalize the process of meeting regularly to not only gripe and complain but also to move into a proactive mood in which we would deal directly with teaching ideas, article reprints, and handouts.

In this level-one gripe session the goal was to try to control concerns by acknowledging them in the presence of others. The climate and atmosphere changed during this "therapy" session. Maybe they had a better handle on their concerns at the end than they did at the beginning. Maybe they were able to read and use some ideas from the article reprints and handouts I left. As I drove back home I knew two things had happened: They had my box of ideas; and they were temporarily feeling a little better.

In a level-two gripe session the goal is to generate some possible actions to deal with some "what's wrong" and "why don't they" issues. An example of this format is to form problem-solving groups in which three to five teachers generate complaints and possible solutions. One way to structure this format is to follow these "griping rules." One teacher is to voice one concern while everyone else listens. Then the other members are to give a possible solution or course of action. The members are not to judge the concern in any way, they are only to give a possible course of action. For example, suppose Jack, a fifth-grade teacher says, "I don't like it when the principal observes me for only one hour and writes up an evaluation." The other teachers are to only generate some possible alternatives like "Ask her to stay the whole morning," or "See if she will coteach a lesson that lasts for a few days." Or suppose, Jill, a first-grade teacher says, "I am concerned about several of my lowest reading students who may be getting discouraged." The other teachers then make suggestions about books, materials, teaching strategies, grouping ideas, and so on that they may know about or have tried that keep children interested and motivated.

The idea behind the griping format is that complaining is natural. Griping reflects a need for a fresh perspective, a cleansing, and a catharsis. Sometimes it helps to only gripe. At other times it is important to generate some possible actions that may eliminate or at least reduce the cause of the irritation. One way to think about this is that frustrations and feelings of failure are often just a lack of alternatives. So even if Jack gets only one idea that helps him with his gripe about the principal, he is ahead. And the same goes for Jill. If she goes back to her lower readers with an alternative she hasn't tried, she has gained something from griping.

Brainstorming

This format has essentially one narrow purpose: to allow ideas and reactions to surface. For this to happen we must take special care to avoid criticism, analysis, and even discussion while ideas surface. The usual procedure is to first select an issue to focus on and then go over the ground rules. These rules are crucial if we want to generate a wide array of ideas and opinions. I often post these rules on a chart or put them on a handout so that we can all read them together.

1. All ideas related to the topic in any direct way are desired.
2. A maximum number of related ideas are desired.
3. One idea may be modified or adapted and expressed as another idea.
4. Ideas should be expressed as clearly and concisely as possible.
5. No discussion and no criticism of any ideas should be attempted.

Arrangements for brainstorming include a group leader for small groups or a recorder and/or an assistant leader for large groups. Groups as small as 2 or as large as 60 or 70 can brainstorm provided two or three leaders are available to record ideas at the same time. Large sheets of paper, an overhead projector, or a chalkboard are useful for recording items. I have found these suggestions to also be helpful:

1. Establish a time limit based on the size of the group and the issue.
2. Encourage and stimulate without being too directive.

3. Restate ideas, but let silence prevail for up to a minute to allow for thinking time.
4. Record each idea so that everyone can refer to it while other ideas are generated.
5. Let ideas flow informally with a minimum of formal recognition of individuals.
6. When interest wavers, or time limits are reached, terminate the session with a review that lets participants see their productiveness.

Follow up the generation of ideas with whole-group discussions or small-group buzz sessions that analyze, edit, revise, and suggest courses of action.

Finally, brainstorming works only when there is a real problem or issue that needs a variety of new ideas. If teachers sense that their ideas will not be used or if the issue only has two alternatives, brainstorming may fizzle out and end in silent frustration. But if a fresh approach is called for and there are no foreseeable restrictions, go ahead and brainstorm.

Role-Playing

With this format one or more people assume roles and spontaneously act out a specified role in an attempt to *act* and *feel* as they might in a real situation. Playing a role for a short time calls for a temporary suspension of reality. The intent is to understand the feelings of others and develop some skills in spontaneous verbal interaction.

The plan is to establish some rapport with an introductory activity, identify a situation, assign roles, act out the role-playing scene, and stop at the appropriate time. Because the level of involvement can be intense, it is important that the participants feel relatively comfortable with the role at the outset. This is best accomplished by directing the *playing* to a very specific problem and giving explicit role assignments. The participants have every right to know what is expected of them. Participants should be cautioned to adhere to their assigned roles, and leaders should be ready to terminate the roles before the *play* (remember, the word is *play*) becomes emotionally embarrassing.

Immediate follow-up is important to seek reactions from the actors and the audience. Buzz sessions, group discussions, or an expert's analysis are often useful follow-up activities. Switching roles is another variation, provided time is taken to contrast the two situations.

It is important for leaders of this format to be sensitive to the actors' feelings. A friendly, permissive, and constructive attitude can go a long way in overcoming embarrassment by the role players.

Productive Formats

In order for you to implement changes in your teaching, you need the time and opportunity to produce agreements and plans and to develop and redesign materials and teaching strategies. True changes require the creation or production of something new or something that didn't exist before. Changing teaching strategies requires repeated tryouts, lots of support from colleagues, and altering lessons to get them to work. Several productive formats that teachers respond to favorably are learning centers, materials production, conferences, and pairs and triads.

Learning Centers

This productive format involves placing new ideas, such as sample lessons, descriptions of teaching strategies, classroom management ideas, and assessment procedures, on tables. Over a one- to two-hour period, teachers move from center to center working through activities that last about 15 to 20 minutes at each table. A large room or several classrooms are used and from 20 to 100 teachers can be involved. A minischedule is used to keep people moving so that everyone has a chance at different centers. For example, one center could contain a sample novel unit and directions for developing novel units. It could also have several novels to look at and paper and pencils so that teachers could look over the samples and attempt to create portions of a new novel unit based on one of the novels at the station. Other centers could have samples and directions for preparing story grammar materials for narrative text and reading guides for expository text. Another type of center may contain some commercial material that teachers could study, react to, and even order if they wanted it for future use.

Learning centers work because teachers have choices and time to pursue new ideas from a hands-on viewpoint. However, they require materials, adequate space, a lot of prior planning and set-up time, and a good selection of both teacher-made and commercial materials.

Material Production

For a long time teachers have commented favorably about sessions that allowed them to change ideas into reality by creating teaching materials, record-keeping systems, and other teaching aids. This format allows teachers to produce useful materials in forms that they will use with students. Some of the typical materials that teachers make include attractive posters and bulletin board displays, learning center materials, teaching-strategy handouts, record-keeping forms, check lists for portfolios, and so on.

This format requires advance planning and a budget for materials and equipment. Poster board, paper, tape, markers, transparencies, staplers, rulers, scissors, and other supplies are arranged for easy access in a suitable working setting. Tables, chairs, copying machines, computers, printers, and cutting boards are basic to a successful "make and take" session.

This format also demands some good models, examples, and construction directions. Very often creative teachers are invited to display their products and give other teachers tips and help. Time is also an important factor, and productive sessions often are from two hours to a whole morning or afternoon.

Conferences

A conference learning format involves arranging times when teachers can meet individually with an instructor, a mentor, a peer teacher, or anyone with whom the teacher feels a need to confer. The key to this format is that the teacher confers only if she or he feels the need. Sometimes this format requires that there be some type of sign-up sheet with dates and names and a private area with a table, desk, and two chairs. Usually conferences are scheduled for 15 to 30 minutes. Sometimes two teachers can confer at a time with one instructor.

Experience with conferences reveals that the conferees' orientation toward one another plays a critical role in determining the outcome. We can predict, for example, that a judgmental, critical, or expert role by one of the conferees may not be as effective as a nondirective, constructive, or counselor role. If someone takes an expert stance the person will tell us what is wrong and give specific instructions on how to improve. Usually a direct, critical, and expert stance narrows the choice of suggestions and can lead to an unpleasant experience for someone who is seeking support. On the other hand, having someone who listens, acknowledges concerns, seeks clarification, and asks for suggested solutions, can be helpful. From this perspective, assistance and even specific solutions are offered, but it is made clear that the teacher who is seeking help is responsible for taking the initiative for making it work in the classroom.

Conferences are a powerful way to help teachers change specific teaching behaviors. The key to a successful conference is a teacher with a genuine need to confer, and an instructor, mentor, or peer who acts more like a counselor than an expert with all the answers.

Although it is not absolutely necessary in every case, some conferences result in a written agreement. These agreements serve as informal contracts that firm up a teacher's commitment to implement a new practice. Often these agreements state how the peer, mentor, or instructor will help the teacher, when they will meet again, and how long the agreement will last.

Pairs and Triads

With this arrangement teachers work with one or two others on a common teaching issue. Teachers can be grouped by grade level, interest in a topic, or even simply matched by counting off. Pairs and triads can be short-lived and meet only during a single session. Or they can become a longer-term team that stays together over a semester or school year.

For one-shot pair arrangements, teachers write names and their concerns, interests, questions on 3x5 cards and are grouped using the cards as a guide. Another way to arrange pairs is simply through a discussion and a listing of topics on a chalkboard. Pairs are formed informally according to the topics listed by the entire group. Pairs can work from 10 to 30 minutes, depending upon the nature of the topic. Sometimes it works to switch topics and partners and cover two or more issues during an hour-long session.

If pairs and triads are all dealing with a single general topic, such as improving reading comprehension, a nice touch is to have each pair produce some type of brief report or plan that is reported back to the entire group. One way to help the participants feel productive is to list what the pairs and triads produced. A copy of this list is made for everyone and they have evidence that they generated some worthwhile responses, answers, and alternatives to their concerns.

Pairs and triads can turn into peer-coaching arrangements that last longer than a few working sessions. In many schools peer coaching is the principle school improvement mechanism. Teachers not only confer, they watch each other teach and give each other feedback on what works and what alterations may improve their teaching. Having the trusted support of colleagues is crucial to successfully overcoming the barriers of risk, uncertainty, and fear that accompany trying out a new teaching techniques for the first time. The success of peer coaching is well documented in the literature on staff development (Brandt, 1987; Showers, 1985).

Summary

These 17 formats are professional techniques, not mere time fillers for use during "released" time. They are intended to serve as a menu that you can use to plan implementation activities. And like a good banquet there is an underlying sequence to their use. The introductory and informative formats could be considered as important appetizers that often appear at the front end of a reading program improvement effort. The decisive, interactive, and productive formats represent the main course of change activities. All together these formats represent ways to provide yourself with a diet of activities that will help you reach some degree of closure about changes you want to make. What about dessert? My hope for you is that these formats may provide three key ingredients to successful imple-mentation: positive support, constructive criticism, and help to re-design or modify materials and your teaching strategies (Vacca and Vacca, 1989, p. 360). There is no guarantee of dessert at this meal. That only comes when you implement a new teaching practice and are satisfied it is an improvement over what you used to do. This chapter completes part one of this text on how to plan and implement improvements in literacy learning. The next three chapters in part two present ideas for making basic changes in curriculum, the community, and school improvement funding.

References

Andrews, T. E., Houston, W. R., and Bryant, B. L. (1981). *Adult learners.* Washing-ton, D.C.: Association of Teacher Educators.

Brandt, R. S. (February 1987). On teachers coaching teachers: A conversation with Bruce Joyce. *Educational Leadership, 44,* 12–17.

Erickson, L. (October 1983). Stop shouting! Use writing to keep group decisions on target. *The Executive Educator, 5,* 34–37.

Fullan, M. G. (1992). School snapshot: Focus on collaborative work culture. *Educational Leadership, 49,* 21–22.

Delbecq, A. L., and Van de Ven, A. H. (1971). A group process model for problem identification and program planning. *Journal of Applied Behavioral Science, 4,* 446–492.

Isaacson, N., and Bamburg, J. (November 1992). Can schools become learning organizations? *Educational Leadership, 50,* 42–44.

Miller, R. H. (1987). A method for choosing among several complex alternatives. *Performance & Instruction, 26,* 37–39.

Moller, G., and Bohning, G. (Spring 1992). Setting reading program priorities. *Journal of Reading Education, 17*(3), 22–28.

Showers, B. (April 1985). Teachers coaching teachers. *Educational Leadership, 42,* 43–48.

Vacca, R. T., and Vacca, J. L. (1989). *Content area reading.* Glenview, Ill.: Scott-Foresman.

Part II

Literacy Leaders

In contrast to the "how to" nature of part one of the text, part two discusses three "what to change" aspects of the literacy context that reaches beyond the school. Chapters 7, 8, and 9 target three key areas of concern that teachers must influence in order to exercise their full professional potential as literacy leaders. The literacy curriculum, community support for literacy, and the financing of literacy improvements are three important features of society that effect literacy. Part II of the text challenges teachers to move out of the classroom and seek to change the curriculum—community—cash connection.

Chapter 7 describes the need for, and value of, a school literacy manual. The literacy document described in this section is simply an operating paper (a constitution) that is constantly referred to and amended when needed. It is a basic tool for curriculum alignment and professional development. Readers are shown how to write and use a manual for their own school following detailed examples and sample sections.

Chapter 8 presents examples of how teachers improve the community literacy base through better home-school communication and parent and business involvement. Business and vocational literacy connections are also highlighted as ways to approach literacy from a community improvement perspective. Readers are provided examples of how parent and community support reduces the risks and barriers that accompany change.

Chapter 9 discusses how teachers change literacy funding practices. Two broad directions for change are discussed: redirecting local school improvement funding; and seeking external grant funding for literacy improvements.

Together, the *"how* to change" processes in part I of the text and the *"what* to change" aspects of literacy programs in part II present a detailed look at what working in the *"middle"* to make changes is like for teachers who are full-fledged professionals.

7

Changing Your Literacy Curriculum

*Probably no professional development activity has as much potential for promoting reflection, clarification, articulation, discussion—and risk—as writing.**

When I am on the road, I have come to count on fast-food franchises for a quick meal. But when I visit schools, I have often eaten excellent food in the local school cafeteria. It seems that school cooks have a good idea of what the local tastes prefer, so they prepare and present a school menu that is both tasty and nutritious. And just as the cooks know what to serve, I believe each school needs a literacy menu that reflects local tastes as well as standards of excellence. Of course, each school has a reading and writing diet that teachers feed to the students every day. And very often what the students get, from year to year and grade to grade, depends on what each individual teacher serves. Without beating the fast-food and school-menu metaphor to death, I want you to think along with me on this. One big change that helps improve reading and writing instruction in many schools is for the staff to write a literacy curriculum manual. Before you say, "Oh, no, not another curriculum guide," bear with me for a bit.

Consider, for example, that every McDonald's franchise operation in the world is guided by a manual that details the philosophy, organiza-

*Roland Barth, 1990. *Improving Schools from Within*, p. 86.

101

tional arrangement, staffing plan, job description, floor plan, equipment, menu, etc. Virtually everything that happens (including how to fill and empty the trash bags) in a McDonald's restaurant is covered in this manual and it is updated frequently. The manual also covers public relations and tells how the restaurant is to support local community activities and have a positive image in the community. The manual is one reason we believe we will get reasonably consistent products and service, no matter if we eat at McDonald's in Moscow, Idaho or Moscow, Russia.

Every Organization Needs One

Now, I think I am right when I say there is a good chance most schools do not have a literacy manual; one that details the philosophy, goals, objectives, organizational plan, staffing, pupil placement, classroom instruction, supervision, support, staff development, and ongoing evaluation of the literacy curriculum. Although schools purchase manuals that tell you how to use the books and materials, there usually is no written description of your school organization, staffing, pupil placement and grading, supervision and staff development policies for reading and language arts. These components of a school literacy program exist, but they are often not codified in a manner that allows either you or the principal to have a clear notion of what the intended outcomes of reading and writing instruction are. The lack of intended outcomes (philosophy, goals, objectives) contributes to, and in some cases promotes, the ongoing debates over which is better—whole language or direct instruction, sight words or phonics, grouping or whole class instruction, basal readers or children's literature, and on and on. These debates have been raging for years, and it is, frankly, tiring to be asked to help settle arguments about *how* to teach reading and writing, when there is no agreement on *what* it is that we want learners to be able to do. At McDonald's they have a clear idea of *what* their outcomes are going to be. They know what their essential purpose is. With this clearly in mind they are able to write a comprehensive manual that describes in detail *how* to reach their goal. And their clear statement of purpose allows them to flourish, grow, change, improve, make money.

Why Have a Local School Manual?

Of course, teaching students is not the same as selling hamburgers. But the point is that McDonald's is organized and articulated—they know what their essential purpose is. On the other hand, we operate school programs without articulated outcomes. If McDonald's were as loosely organized as many school literacy curricula are, you might go to one cash register and not be able to get a Big Mac because that person has a different philosophy and serves only Quarter Pounders! We can no longer justify or accept round-robin oral reading as an effective way to use content textbooks, in light of what we know about expository text structure and how reading strategies work. We no longer can accept outdated practices, in light of the many effective practices that are used in enlightened schools by effective teachers. Writing a manual that reflects the best practices in reading and writing instruction is a way for you to see that all students get the best instruction currently available. Writing a local statement is also a way for you to gain control over your own situation, gain a voice, and reduce ambiguity. Because many schools have no shared agreements about literacy, the development of a manual is, in every respect, a significant change.

The work of writing a manual is another example of teachers working "in the middle" to effect changes and improvements. This work represents a significant change and illustrates how teachers become true professionals. But the task of writing a manual is difficult. Reaching shared agreements among teachers, within and across grade levels, is risky, given the tendency for teachers to operate independently from each other. I realize that even after seeing the examples and arguments I've provided, you may not want to attempt to write a reading manual. The next section reflects on this and is intended to motivate you to keep going.

No Voice, No Tolerance for Ambiguity

One of the reasons fast-food places such as McDonald's prosper is that the work is relatively simple and there is low ambiguity for the employees and customers. We can predict with a lot of consistency what to expect either as a worker or as a customer. On the other hand, teaching is complex and plagued by ambiguity. There are teacher manuals, policies, mandates, and a host of sources giving conflicting and mixed messages. Teachers have learned to keep quiet about this, because messages tend to move down from the top much more easily than they move up. (Do you write weekly memos to the principal?) And all of this means you may feel you really do not have a voice. You have also learned that "playing it safe" is how to tolerate all the ambiguity. All of this builds a feeling of powerlessness that has been well documented. For example, Heller (1989) recalls how experienced teachers responded in amazement to her question about their power to change things.

"But why can't you just close your doors and teach the way you really want to teach," I asked naively with a smile on my face. They smiled back at me, checked for microphones hidden in the overhead ceiling fans, and said, "Because we're afraid" (p. 156).

One of the ways you can overcome this fear and reduce ambiguity is to write a local school literacy manual that "voices" both student literacy outcomes and effective teacher practices. A local manual is a first step for teachers who seek to gain professional control. The development of such a manual is evidence that you are true professionals, not just workers who are controlled by superiors who take care of you and tell you what to do. So if you are still with me on this, here is what you might develop. I think when you take a good look at what follows you might feel like trying this.

What Does a Manual Look Like?

You can help your school write a "McDonald's" literacy manual that fits your particular school. This curriculum manual will have something like the following sections. In each section, sample statements from a fictitious Peach Valley School are shown to illustrate what each part can contain.

Part 1 Introduction

This section is brief and describes the school, the community, the neighborhood, the students, the larger literacy context that makes the school unique. Here is an example:

Peach Valley School is one of three elementary schools in the community. It contains three classes each of kindergarten through grade five, with an enrollment of about 350 students. Peach Valley is located approximately 20 miles southeast of Fleming, a city of 100,000. Fleming is the home of several industries, including a new auto assembly plant, as well as the state university. Many teachers and administrators have degrees from the university, and sometimes graduate classes for teachers are offered off campus in Peach Valley.

Peach Valley is an integrated middle-class community of 10,000. Many residents commute to Fleming; others work in in local businesses. The area at one time was a fruit orchard center, and while the peach orchards are now smaller, there are still some that remain in business. The school is located in a hilly area that once was an orchard but is now a residential area that is about 20 years old.

Student achievement is average to above average on local and state tests. Parents are somewhat conservative and expect schools to be orderly, clean, and safe. Reading and writing programs in the schools are considered to be adequate, although local funding problems have limited the purchase of some materials and equipment.

Part 2 Philosophy and Reading Program Goals

This part is very important because it describes what the overall school reading and writing program is trying to accomplish in terms of teacher and student behaviors. Look at your state or district curriculum guide and see how this is done. Here is an example based on the *Wisconsin Guide to Curriculum Planning*, pages 6 and 7 (Cook, 1986).

Peach Valley School Reading Program

We believe reading is first and foremost comprehending. Reading comprehension is an interactive process in which readers construct meaning by combining their existing knowledge with the text information within the context of the reading situation. The key components of the reading process are the reader, the text, and the context.

I. Our major goal in reading is to develop strategic readers who understand how reading works and who can:
   A. Construct meaning from print
   B. Apply strategies to learn from text
   C. Develop an interest and lifelong enjoyment for reading

II. We want students to become strategic readers who can:
   A. Analyze a reading task and establish a purpose
   B. Plan appropriate reading strategies and monitor understanding while reading
   C. Regulate their reading and make appropriate corrections
   D. Reflect and apply understandings upon completion of reading

III. As teachers we are professional decision makers who decide how and what to teach and we believe:
   A. Effective reading instruction is student centered so we build upon what students know
   B. We can best teach by using a variety of materials
   C. We must model appropriate reading by:
      1. demonstrating reading strategies
      2. reading aloud to students

    3. encouraging students to interact about what they are reading

D. An effective reading program is more than basal readers and workbooks. It includes:

    1. a variety of narrative and expository material
    2. self-selected reading by all students

E. Comprehension is the main event of reading and the goal of word analysis is meaning

F. Effective reading lessons feature before or prereading activities, active thinking during reading, and postreading activities that examine and apply information

G. Reading is the best practice for learning to read so we encourage:

    1. silent reading
    2. reading for enjoyment
    3. fun activities that develop positive reading attitudes

IV. As professionals we believe:

A. Staff Development is essential to our reading program so that we will:

    1. keep abreast of new insights about teaching reading
    2. continually upgrade reading materials
    3. continually work together to improve our program

These outcome statements are crucial and can be used as criteria for making all of the detailed decisions about *how* to proceed. These behaviors are also the basis for evaluating strengths and weaknesses of the program, and can lead to program improvement and staff development activities that focus directly on both long-term and everyday concerns.

Part 3 Organization, Staffing, Placement

This section describes how the school is organized to teach reading and writing. Staffing patterns, time schedules, school policies, special classes, volunteers, grading, and other organizational practices are described in detail. Here is a sample of the plan at Peach Valley School.

Peach Valley teachers in self-contained classrooms usually form three or more reading groups. Reading is taught for 90 minutes each day in grades 1–3 and 60 minutes daily in grades 4–5. In the primary grades, each teacher has a parent aide and some use older students from grade 5 to help with special programs. Classes are heterogeneously grouped, although some poorer readers go to special reading (a Chapter One program) and others go to a Gifted program during reading. Students are tested using the magazine tests that accompany the basal reading series. The school also gives a standardized reading test to assist with grouping decisions.

Part 4 Classroom Reading Instruction

This section shows the progression of reading and writing objectives, teacher activities, and student behaviors that flow from grade to grade. These are extensions of the general outcomes described in part two of this manual. This section can also describe the materials used, the record-keeping system, and evaluation processes and products teachers use at each grade level. Here is a sample of a first-grade format that is adapted from Cook (1986) and deals only with reading.

	Grade	Teacher Activities	Student Behaviors
Word Level Meaning	First	Teaches high frequency words.	Uses high frequency words automatically in writing.
Word Analysis	First	Teaches integration of phonics, structural, and contextual analysis.	Associates sound with letters in words for beginning and ending consonants.
Text Level Narrative	First	Teaches story map terminology/concepts.	Uses story structure terms in speaking about stories.
Expository	First	Reads and provides informational books for students to read.	Listens, reads, asks questions.
Critical Reading and Thinking	First	Teaches criteria for identifying a good story.	Compares stories and expresses a preference.
Responding in Writing	First	Encourages students to write on their own.	Describes pictures with phrases or sentences. Composes simple stories using invented spelling.
Attitudes and Interests	First	Provides reading corner with interesting books.	Uses free time to browse and read independently.

Part 5 Supervision, Administrative Support

This section describes the leadership and organizational structures that exist for literacy programs in the school. Is there a reading resource teacher, is there a committee, is there a person who provides direction, coordination for the literacy curriculum? Does the school subscribe to teacher journals? The support from the district central office is also described, as is the schoolwide program evaluation. Staff development is described in this section, and budget policies for the operation and ongoing growth of the program are detailed here. Here is an example from the Peach Valley School.

> The Peach Valley School principal is the primary supervisor of instruction who observes teachers and makes overall judgments about their teaching. There is no special reading supervisor, although the regional superintendent's office does have specialists who are available upon request. Most support is in the form of a budget for materials, and the administration does hire speakers for schoolwide staff development meetings that occur about four times a year. Teachers have input by filling out questionnaires or recommending good speakers they have heard about to the administration. There is support for one day of teacher visitation to other classrooms. Sometimes a consultant from a publisher is available to help implement the basal reading material. For the most part the teachers are experienced veterans who are trusted and expected to teach quite well without much supervision.

Writing a Local Literacy Manual

Are you still with me? If you think your school has a need for a manual to help guide the school reading and writing program, here is a step-by-step plan to follow. The leadership for this task is ideally a well-informed principal or reading specialist who believes in the value of having reasonable and attainable outcomes to guide the organization. However, in many schools, teachers like you successfully lead the writing team with the direct support of someone in an administrative/supervisory role. This is a time-consuming task that will take a year at the minimum to make some progress.

Step 1

Form a writing team of teachers and employ them during the summer, or give them released time to work during the year. The team will need to examine existing documents, such as local school district manuals, state and regional curriculum guides. If no reading and language arts specialists are readily available, give the team a budget to hire a knowledgeable consultant who can provide some technical help with the writing and editing. Team members should represent a variety of grades and have about six weeks to work. An excellent model to start with is *A Guide to Curriculum Planning in Reading,* by Doris Cook (1986). It is published by the Wisconsin Department of Public Instruction, Madison, Wisconsin. Another starting point is to use state education outcomes. For example, the Illinois State Board of Education (1990) has outcomes in reading and language arts for grades 3, 6, 8, and 11 that are part of state law and give an overview of goals and sample learner outcomes that will guide the team's writing.

Step 2

The first task of the team is to read and study existing material, such as that listed above in step one. Talk over the material, ask questions, interview each other, and get input from teachers, administrators, the community, and a literacy specialist who knows something about the local community. This early dialogue gives everyone a chance to share what they know, state their position, and get to know each other. The first two meetings of the team should be exploratory in nature and employ activities such as brainstorming, buzz sessions, and open-ended activities. The goal of these initial meetings is to become a team with members who have had a chance to tell who they are and what they want the manual to be like. This early teamwork is usually messy and noisy, and there is some conflict as people try to influence each other. But out of this initial messiness comes the ability to predict each other's styles and positions on issues. And this prediction leads to trust.

Step 3

The next task is to begin to reach consensus on literacy outcomes for students. The team tries to write answers to questions such as: What do we want students' reading and writing behaviors and attitudes to be at various grade levels? Many existing materials (books, curriculum guides, text manuals, etc.) describe these. The team's task is to write some statements that reflect what they want students to be like as a result of what teachers do over succeeding grade levels. In Illinois these outcomes are part of the state code for schools. For example, a team in Illinois would find the following language arts goals for grades 3, 6, 8, and 11.

Reading: Students will be able to read, comprehend, interpret, evaluate, and use written materials.

Listening: Students will be able to listen critically and analytically.

Writing: Students will be able to write standard English in a grammatical, well-organized, and coherent manner for a variety of purposes.

Speaking: Students will be able to use spoken language effectively in formal and informal situations to communicate ideas and information and to ask and answer questions.

Step 4

The next task is to write scope and sequence statements that describe the student level or age and the teacher and student behaviors and activities that will lead up to the written outcomes agreed to in the preceding step. The general outline for a scope and sequence grid is like the first-grade example presented in part four of the preceding section.

The team should write outcomes for each grade that are reasonable and not too lengthy or detailed. A good rule of thumb is to have no more than eight to ten outcomes for each goal for each grade. All teachers should have input to this so that the outcomes are supported by the staff. Of course, this is easier said than done, but experience with this process can yield a product the teachers will find very helpful for gaining support from both within the school system and across the community.

Next, the manual needs descriptions of teacher behaviors and teaching strategies that fit with these outcomes. Again, the Wisconsin guide (Cook, 1986) is a good model to look at for this part of the manual. This information comes from existing practices, manuals, texts, and would reflect not only existing practices that are known to be effective but also new practices yet to be implemented. The team should now be able to write the first two sections of the manual.

Step 5

At this point the manual is actually an ideal description of the literacy plan for the school. As such it serves as a guide for both *describing* and *assessing* the next three portions of a comprehensive school literacy plan. In other words, as the team describes the school organization plan, the staffing pattern, and the pupil placement (Part 3), the classroom reading instruction (Part 4), and the supervision and administrative support (Part

5), you will feel tempted to use two types of information. Should you describe the *actual,* or current program components, or the future *ideal* components? The answer is that you should do *both.* For example, when you discuss the school organization plan, you probably will encounter a variety of organizational plans within your school. A good way to proceed is to use a format that allows you to describe the current plan, and also discuss future directions for possible improvement. Here is a common format for doing this:

School/Classroom Organizational Plan, Staffing, and Pupil Placement for Teaching Reading, Writing, Speaking, and Listening

School: Peach Valley
Grade: 3

Current Plan
Teachers in self-contained classrooms form three or more reading groups. Reading is taught for 90 minutes each day. Each teacher has a parent aide and some use older students from grade 5 to help with special programs. Classes are heterogeneously grouped, although some poorer readers go to special reading (a Chapter One program) and others go to a Gifted program during reading. Students are tested using the magazine tests that accompany the basal reading series. The school also gives a standardized reading test to assist with grouping decisions.

Future Plan
Some teachers are interested in combining all the language arts into a two-hour block of time to allow more integration of reading, writing, spelling, speaking, listening. They are also interested in having better communication and coordination with the Chapter One and Gifted programs. Some teachers are using checklists and pupil conferences for evaluation purposes. One teacher is using reading portfolios to collect data on students' interests, habits, and written responses to reading. Other teachers are interested in learning more about portfolios. Two teachers are trying out cooperative learning groups.

Classroom Reading Instruction

School: Peach Valley
Grade: 3

Current Instruction
All teachers currently use a tribasal reading series so that the high group uses Scott Foresman, the middle groups use Houghton Mifflin, and the low group uses Addison Wesley. Some additional supplementary workbooks are used to reinforce phonics and vocabulary skills.

Future Instruction
Some teachers are experimenting with more literature-based and sustained silent reading activities one or two days per week. These approaches are more whole-class oriented, and teachers are concerned about changing from the three group plan to the whole-class plan. Some teachers are using reading comprehension strategies and combining literature and content area text materials.

Supervision and Administrative Support

School: Peach Valley
Grade: 3

Current Support
The principal is the supervisor of instruction who observes teachers and makes overall judgments about their teaching. There is no special reading supervisor, although the regional superintendent's office does have specialists who are available upon request. Most support is in the form of a budget for materials, and the administration does hire speakers for schoolwide staff development meetings that occur about four times a year. Teachers have input by filling out questionnaires or recommending good speakers they have heard about to the administration. There is support for one day of teacher visitation to other classrooms. Sometimes a consultant from a publisher is available to help implement the basal reading material. For the most part, teachers are experienced veterans who are trusted and expected to teach quite well without much supervision.

Future Support
Several teachers are currently working together with some parents to promote more reading/writing at home. The principal is most supportive of this idea, and there are plans to expand the home reading and writing project to the entire school. There has been some dissatisfaction with a past reading staff development program on whole language, and the staff wants to know more about this idea. Several teachers are taking classes to earn a graduate degree, and they are interested in more time for bottom-up staff development. They say they have some good language arts teaching ideas that would help the entire school.

Step 6

Congratulations. You should celebrate, for you have started using a manual to guide decision making about materials, testing, pupil placement, teaching methods, and on and on. Copies can be used to disseminate information to parents. New teachers can refer to the manual for guidance. Teachers and principals can use it for both daily lesson planning and making longer-range school improvement and staff development decisions. Of course, the manual will need to be updated and changed, so plan to review it periodically—like every three years or so. This manual is really an operating paper that serves as a constitution for governing your school literacy community. Who knows, with such a manual you may be tempted to franchise your literacy program.

Summary

Developing a literacy manual is a way for teachers to grow professionally and exercise their true political power as change agents. Writing is a good way to gain a true voice, for you will have to network with others and read professional journals. You may also have to seek out support and guidance from your college teachers as well as your principal and other officials. Developing written student outcomes and teacher behaviors reduces ambiguity for teachers. A literacy manual can also be used to guide long-range efforts to both personal growth for teachers and organizational excellence for a school. Steps for writing a literacy manual were described and sample sections were provided using actual statements from Wisconsin and Illinois State Educational Agency documents. The next chapter moves beyond the school curriculum and presents ways that teachers and principals improve the school-community literacy connection.

References

Barth, R. (1990). *Improving schools from within.* San Francisco: Jossey-Bass Publishing.

Cook, D. (1986). *A guide to curriculum planning in reading.* Madison: Wisconsin Department of Public Instruction. Bulletin No. 6305.

Heller, M. F. (1989). Developing a tolerance for ambiguity. In Hayes, B., and Camperell, K. (Eds.), *Reading researchers, policy makers, and practitioners.* American Reading Forum Yearbook, Volume IX.

Illinois goal assessment program (December 1990). Illinois State Board of Education, 100 North First Street, Springfield, Ill. 62777.

8

Changing School-Community Literacy Connections

The new level of professionalism . . . , [and] the new type of accountability that is developing around it, could not exist without the new relationships with parents, students, and the community. At these two schools, learning about the community and how to work with it is an important part of staff development.*

In my former life as an elementary principal, I was often asked by young parents to recommend neighborhoods with the "best" schools. Of course, I made a pitch for the school where I worked, but I often told them to check out the schools with the highest reading scores. My reason for this is simple. It makes sense to send children to a school in a neighborhood where reading and writing are valued. Going to school where "everyone" learns to read and write usually means that literacy expectations are high not only in the school. Communities with high literacy expectations will expect the school to deliver, and the parents, extended families, businesses, and services in the area will also deliver. There will be a richer environment of materials, as well as a context where print is valued and used. Perhaps one of the reasons New Zealand has a high level of literacy

---

*David Seeley, 1989. *A New Paradigm for Parent Involvement*, p. 47.

was expressed by a young New Zealand parent who quipped, "I thought it was against the law not to have a library card."

The family and community role in literacy learning is well documented, and serves to remind us once again about the power of the social context for reading and writing. The first social context for reading and writing is the home. And in this setting, reading and writing can be "natural, pleasurable, and highly practical" (Piazza and Tomlinson, 1985). The neighborhood and community is also an important setting for literacy. I recall that, like a lot of other children, my own early social setting for reading and writing was practical.

It included my grandmother, Franklin School, and the Carnegie Library. At home I have dim memories of grandmother Hulda reading aloud to me from thick books without many pictures. At Franklin School my early reading and writing efforts were guided by teachers like Miss Jacobson, Mrs. Marino, and Miss Barr. The high-ceiling classrooms in those days provided a social setting in which those teachers stood immediately over me. And above them, high on the walls, George Washington and Abraham Lincoln listened to us read.

But another feature of this social setting I vividly recall is the public library. The red-stone Carnegie library was on the same block as Franklin School, and I can visualize (and smell) the basement area that housed the children's books. I even remember that the John R. Tunis books were on the south wall under the little window near the ceiling. I believe the reason I discovered authors so early is related to winter weather and lunch hours. Everyone, except a few bus children, walked home, and we were not supposed to return to the playground after lunch until ten minutes before the afternoon bell. So when it was cold, we headed for the basement library room where steam radiators could protect us until the school doors opened. Of course, the librarian had to protect her domain during this time. But overall it was fortunate that I was close to so many books on practically a daily basis. And I am convinced that this early natural, pleasurable, and practical social setting is the reason I continue to value libraries, reading, and writing. Of course, this was a long time ago, before television, reading specialists, state tests, and the whole mix of criticism and hope about reading and writing that surrounds teachers today.

Reading and Writing as School Work: The Narrow View

Today, the social setting and the value placed on literacy in our communities may not foster a natural and practical reading and writing setting.

And this lack of a natural setting for literacy is not limited to homes where we currently label the children to be "at risk." In far too many schools and communities, reading and writing are viewed primarily as school "work" where the "product" is test scores. For me, this narrow view of literacy is easy to trace. I recall consulting with a statewide Right To Read program in the 1970s that featured a skills-based approach. The state had money to buy skill lists for every teacher and tests for every elementary child. But in some schools they did not have enough reading textbooks for each child and no school or community library. When I reminded them that the state ranked near the bottom nationally in libraries, and that a state-wide literacy effort ought to address this need, they stuck to their skills viewpoint. Perhaps my question to them, "Why teach reading skills when there is nothing to read?" was a bit harsh. But a large-scale skills-based program is not natural, pleasurable, or practical.

What accounts for this narrow view of literacy as school "work?" I think it has something to do with the fact that schools are state agencies that are accountable to legislative pressures. And because these pressures are political, they are often narrowly focused and short-range. For example, in the 1980s a state governor was prepared to spend $40 million on reading improvement. He was going to announce in his state-of-the-state address that most of the money ($32 million) was to be spent on hiring a reading aide for every first grade in the state. Different consultants were asked to review the plan, make some comments, and forward them back to the governor's education adviser. As one of the consultants, I said that spending almost all of the money on first grade was a nice idea that would make a lot of first-grade teachers happy. But it was too narrow. I recommended that the state should spend the money on instructional and library materials, and staff development on a K to 12 basis, so that all students might benefit. Apparently other consultants had similar opinions, and the governor's original plan was altered. Money for materials and staff development was provided to fund a state reading improvement effort with a much broader perspective than the original first-grade aide plan.

The point of all of this is that current top-down literacy efforts by state and local educational agencies have a tendency to be heavy on school testing and accountability efforts. The effects of mandates, testing, and all the pressures to raise reading achievement have caused us to put too much emphasis on vocabulary and comprehension scores. The need for accountability and immediate results creates "culture-bound ways of thinking, problem solving, and engaging the world" (Bloome, 1985, p. 139). Culture-bound thinking continues to produce top-down literacy mandates that emphasize massive school accountability efforts. All of this has caused us to confuse the things that are countable—such as vocabulary and comprehension scores, with the things that count—such as reading to complete important tasks and reading for enjoyment. The test-score view of reading and writing is a narrow view that teachers are changing.

Reading and Writing As Community Improvement: A Wider View

In this chapter I want to show how teachers are reminding us that improving reading and writing involves more than a school effort to improve test scores. A broader literacy perspective means that the grassroots community-based efforts of local teachers and principals have more impact than mandated top-down, test-oriented literacy activities. In a recent spirited teacher discussion in a graduate literacy seminar, one teacher said it well: "We need a massive *community accountability* effort, not just a school or teacher accountability program, to improve reading and writing." In this chapter I present the view that teachers and principals are change agents who improve community accountability for literacy learning by focusing on two concerns: trust between parents and teachers on literacy issues; and business and vocational literacy partnerships. Like the other chapters in this section of the text, the focus is more on *what* to change than *how* to change. The intent is that the strategies presented in the first section of this text are the "how to" part. The ideas in this chapter represent two of any number of possible directions to follow to close gaps that may exist between school and community literacy viewpoints and practices.

Teachers Change Parent/Home Literacy Connections

Communicate to Build Trust

Every teacher communicates with parents through notes sent home, by occasional telephone calls, at open houses, and at conference times. But very often this communication is formal, stilted, and even technical. And sometimes "good news" is shared. But far too much teacher-parent communication is based on a "what's wrong" attitude. As a principal, I recall coaxing a mother to school to share her son's improved behavior and improved reading and writing. Her response was, "No, sir, I'm not coming. Every time I go over there all I ever hear is bad news." And as a parent, I remember calling my daughter's excellent teacher. I wanted to meet her, compliment her, and perhaps share some teaching ideas. When she picked up the phone, I told her who I was and her first response was, "What's wrong?" I said, "Nothing is wrong, I like what you are doing and want to talk about good teaching ideas."

I share these experiences because I know there is a tendency for teachers and parents to mistrust each other. And trust is perhaps the most powerful determinant of home-school relationships. For example, at an open house way back in 1962, I was having a cup of coffee with a father who said, "The reason I'm here tonight is that I'm really not interested in those books and what you are teaching as much as I am curious about what kind of person you are and how you'll treat my child." The bottom line is that parents want teachers they can trust. And trust is a subtle phenomenon that is difficult to explain because of the complicated interaction that nurtures its existence. So rather than unraveling all of the theory, consider that trust is built when teachers can predict parent reactions to school practices, and parents can accurately predict school policies, procedures, and teacher behaviors. The key idea in all of this is *prediction*. For, in order to predict each other's responses, teachers and parents need to communicate often and openly about both positive and negative issues. Both parties have to experience success in predicting each other's responses in both good and bad situations. Frequent, accurate, and successful prediction experiences by teachers and parents are absolutely necessary to establish and maintain a trusting relationship. And this takes a long time. One or two attempts to meet with parents will not be enough. A trust-building effort must be measured in months, semesters, and years of frequent formal and informal meetings in school, at homes, and in various community settings.

Teachers who take the initiative to build trust treat parents as partners and *coequals* (Losen and Diament, 1978). They know that assuming parents don't want to interact as equals will become a self-fulfilling prophecy; so they treat parents as partners and build productive, student-centered relationships. Here are some things the most trusted teachers and principals do to overcome the anxieties that plague parent-teacher relationships.

1. Instead of assuming they are authorities who have all of the answers, principals and teachers listen to parents and let parents know that there may be a middle ground for agreement and that compromise and mutual support are possible. A win-win outcome is better than a win-lose stalemate.

2. Instead of denying any faults, principals and teachers admit to mistakes and let parents know they are willing to learn from them. Teachers relate their teaching shortcomings in a way that helps parents realize they are not alone with their parenting shortcomings.

3. Instead of using jargon they use easily understood terms, and give parents opportunities to stop the conversation and ask for clarification.
4. Instead of viewing the parent as having all the concerns and the teacher as having all the answers, teachers encourage parents to suggest solutions. Teachers let parents reflect on suggestions so that mutual agreement is possible.
5. Instead of labeling children, teachers focus on the behaviors. John is not called a poor reader. Rather, the teacher gives an exact description of his reading rate that characterizes his word-by-word oral reading. The teacher then shares how she and the parent can both help improve his fluency.

The idea of equalizing the roles of both teachers and parents is also supported by Lingle (1989). Her study of parent preferences reveals that regardless of socioeconomic status, families preferred teachers to be "personal" rather than "professional." Parents were dissatisfied when school people were "too businesslike," "patronizing," or "talk down to us" (p. 13). Parents preferred regular, immediate, and informal talk such as phone calls or personal notes. They disliked a formal "professional-client" relationship (p. 14). Parents viewed ten minute scheduled conferences with skepticism. The short time was perceived as a way for the teacher, as the professional, to dominate the parent, who is the client. As one parent said, "I need time to tell the teacher about how my child is at home, too" (p. 14).

Teachers who realize how personal communication builds and maintains trusting home-school partnerships go beyond the typical scheduled conference and the formal open house. Here is a sample of what they do:

1. At least one or two "good news" notes are sent home or phone calls are made to families each week. The principal also does this on a regular basis.
2. Informal teacher and parent meetings are held in homes. Small groups meet, share refreshments, discuss general literacy issues.
3. Teachers make individual home visits to learn about their students and discuss specific literacy issues.
4. Individual teachers have their own parent meetings at school frequently throughout the year.
5. Children are sent to the principal's office for doing well or for showing improvement.
6. Children are present, when appropriate, for conferences.
7. Portfolios documenting student literacy growth are regularly shared with families.

8. Conferences for all students are arranged. Having conferences for only those who "need" them is strictly an adversary policy that breeds estrangement between home and school.

In addition to telephone and face-to-face communication, teachers also initiate effective written communication such as:

1. Newsletters that tell of school events are sent home every week. Items help families predict upcoming events and also report recent happenings.
2. Clearly written explanations of school teaching practices, homework policies, or suggestions for home studying are sent home to let parents predict what the school expects. The most useful explanations are often written by a committee of teachers and parents.
3. A teacher writes a weekly column in the local newspaper that shares timely and positive literacy information for parents.

Celebrate Literacy to Highlight the Good News

In much the same manner that school athletic events are celebrations, additional activities are planned by teachers to celebrate literacy and other academic student performance. This is important in light of all of the negative news items about how schools are failing. I remember the headline that said "Parents Reject Gifted Program." The newspaper story went on to talk about reasons four parents did not want their children involved in activities for gifted and talented students. Buried in the middle of the story was the fact that 168 children were involved. To offset the negative news about teaching we need to actively publicize the good news. Here is a sample of how teachers and principals validate the good things that students (and parents) do week in and week out.

1. School principal Davis (1989) reported how each week teachers pick two students who get ribbons in honor of their reading and writing efforts. The ribbons are donated by the PTA and are awarded at an assembly every Friday morning. In his school there are 21 rooms so 42 ribbons per week add up to 1,470 a year. Parents are also called in the evenings or even on weekends to explain the award. These phone calls are done in different languages by teachers and community members. Davis says that if a child attends the school for seven years the chances are you will get at least 7 to 14 positive calls during that time. And this goes a long way in validating good parental skills.
2. Teachers arrange a ceremony to celebrate the adoption of new reading materials. The mayor, PTA, board of education, the superintendent,

as well as the adoption committee, are present for a "book-opening" ceremony much like a"ground-breaking" or a "ribbon-cutting."

3. An all day "read-a-thon" or "read-in" is held, and adults such as the sheriff, or the chief of police, or other officials and business people come to school to read to the students. Often special areas are arranged in the school (tents, a clear plastic air-supported dome, floor mats, lofts, and other interesting reading spaces) and students rotate from place to place reading their current favorite choice. Numbers of pages read, or the total number of books read, are recorded to set goals for future efforts. Activities like this are often videotaped, shared with other schools, and used to publicize the community support for literacy.

4. Principal William Griffin (1988) reported how a Read Aloud Week is an annual school-community event that features ingenious and creative presentations. One reader wrote an original horse story, and the horse came to school when the story was read. And the horse wore glasses and had a book bag on his back. A police officer read to second graders from the back of the police wagon. And a parish priest led kindergarten singing as a prereading activity. The local cable TV company taped readers each day and showed an hour's worth each night.

5. Student writing is celebrated by publishing (editing, binding) student stories. Parents help in the editing and binding, and student books are placed in the school library. Writing contests (poetry, short stories, reporting, cartoons, etc.) are held monthly, winners receive ribbons, and their names, pictures, and writings are published in the local paper.

In addition to publicizing and celebrating good literacy practices, positive school and community connections are being made by teachers who break down the walls between the classroom and the community.

Teachers Tap Community Talent Sources

One definition says a teacher is usually a female who works alone all day with a distillation of the community. While there is some truth to this view, there are teachers who do not always work alone. They have learned to tap the talents of the local community, and the result is an enriched literacy environment. And while there seems to be a move to open schools to involve parents and volunteers, I recall a veteran elementary principal telling me what he did to "keep parents and other troublemakers away." There sometimes seems to be a belief that teachers and parents don't mix. Why did he feel his job involved doing this? I suspect he felt he was protecting himself and the teachers from some hassles and criticism. I agree that protecting and defending comes with the territory called principal, but being too defensive breeds mistrust and alienation.

The result of a strong defensive view toward parents and volunteers is usually an adversary gap. There is little trust when, like two armies peering over a truce line, school and community only interact when a violation is reported. And since there is a better-than-even chance that a report may be rumor or a genuine mistake, the truce zone widens and the two camps move farther apart, trusting each other even less than before.

In order to prevent or close existing gaps, and to enrich and extend the literacy curriculum, teachers and principals turn to the community. They do so because they believe that to overlook the knowledge and skills which parents and other volunteers possess shortchanges students. For example, Hunter (1989) describes how teachers identified four kinds of volunteer competencies:

1. Skills associated with hobbies and crafts.

2. Knowledge and experience associated with occupations.

3. Knowledge, skills, and an appreciation associated with different cultures.

4. Helping out skills associated with being an "extra hand" at school for instructional, clerical, or supervisory tasks.

To enlist help, teachers sent letters to parents and other people in the community that invited them to describe just how they might help. A model letter (adapted for literacy enrichment) might look like this:

```
Dear _____

     We are seeking to tap your talents, abilities, and interests in
order to enrich our school literacy curriculum. We would like to poll
your interest and availability to participate at school in the
following areas. This is in no way an obligation, just an
opportunity.
1. Knowing and valuing cultural differences. We know that a rich
variety of literacy activities are based on the cultures of all of
the peoples of the world. Could you share your special nationality or
ethnic knowledge through storytelling, music, special books, or
another language or alphabet?
```

❏ **Yes   My special cultural interest is** _____

_____

```
     I could contribute by presenting:
     ____folklore and literature,    ____ music,          ____art,
     ____special books,              ____ oral language,
     ____writing/alphabet,           ____ other:
```

2. <u>Arts, Crafts, and Hobbies</u>. Many of you engage in art, craft, and hobby activities. Could you share your special talent and interest and show how speaking, reading, and writing are related to the enjoyment of this activity?

❑ **Yes**   **I could share my interest in** _____

_____

3. <u>The World of Work</u>. Hearing and seeing how reading and writing relate to "real" jobs and occupations is important for students. Could you talk about this and show examples of the literacy activities that are important to your work?

❑ **Yes**   **I could tell about and bring examples of how reading and writing relate to** _____

_____

_____

4. <u>The "short-handed" school</u>. Sometimes we need help with instructional materials, clerical chores, or even supervising students. Could you be an extra pair of hands?

❑ **Yes**   **I would be willing to** _____

_____

_____

Involving parents and other community volunteers in school literacy learning is imperative if reading and writing are to flourish in a community. The preceding information and activities show some of the ways teachers and principals reach out to build community-based accountability. Such proactive efforts go a long way beyond the tendency to sit back in a reactive stance and "blame" others for low literacy expectations. In schools where teachers and principals build family- and community-based literacy efforts, the payoff usually does not come fast, nor are simple one-shot efforts effective. A reasonable time line is that it will take from two to five years to significantly close the adversary gaps that often exist between schools and parents.

Finally, there simply is no excuse today for not knowing what to do to involve parents. A wealth of ideas on parent involvement is available from many sources. Perhaps the best recent example I know of is the monthly parent involvement column in the 1990 to 1992 editions of *The Reading Teacher,* published by the International Reading Association. Column editors Tim Rasinsky and Tony Fredericks provided readers with many workable ideas. They also can send you more. For a free guide to over 60 ideas, ask for "Success Tips From Successful Parent Involvement

Programs" from Anthony D. Fredericks, Department of Education, York College, York, PA 17403.

Community-Based Business and Vocational Literacy Connections

Many reading and writing school efforts in the 1990s are basing instruction on "whole-language" concepts that feature high-quality literature. The rationale for this is most sound, because good literature features characters, events, problems, and outcomes that reflect our basic human needs and fears. Good literature has a natural appeal that helps students care about what they read. Another part of the whole-language trend is to have students learn writing as a process that features rewriting, reflections, editing, and publishing. And this, too, is seen to be effective, as students care about writing about their own thoughts and experiences.

However, using good literature, and having students experience writing as authors, is a very school-oriented and one-sided view of literacy. Good literature and authoring is, after all, artwork. And while basing school activities around artistic works taps the natural "storytelling" sense in humans, we must not ignore the vast array of reading and writing that is associated with out-of-school and workplace literacy. There is much to be said for being motivated by experiencing how reading and writing apply in the adult world of work. Home, community and workplace literacy has a place in school, especially in the middle and upper grades.

One way teachers make literacy learning more natural and practical is through the use of materials from the workplace. Teachers work with parents, businesses, and services to gather materials that workers encounter on a daily basis. These materials are read, studied, discussed, and used for homework assignments that are related to everyday community jobs and services.

Materials That Connect Schools and Communities

First of all we need to remember that as teachers we are limited. We can never prepare our students for all of the workplace literacy demands. Job literacy needs change over time; they vary from job to job, and from one location to another. In addition, the classroom and school cannot duplicate the wide variety of specific workplace contexts that affect reading and writing on the job. At work, readers and writers have specific tasks and audiences in mind. What teachers can do, according to Mikulecky (1989), is to model some workplace literacy situations using "a wide variety of materials from newspapers, pamphlets, instructions, forms, announcements, manuals, tables, graphs, charts, advertisements, and correspondence" (p. 130). He suggests the following ways that you can involve your students and the community in making literacy relevant to the world of work.

Gather Materials. Let student teams write letters to and visit businesses and request materials. Have students visit businesses and services and interview managers about job place literacy demands. Have students write instructions to other students who missed assignments. Involve students in school paperwork, such as record keeping and form filling. Have students locate, collect, skim/read current periodicals and newspapers for work-related topics.

Use Literacy for Problem Solving. Have students write letters about product information. Let students plan detailed trips by reading maps and travel guides to figure lodging, food, travel, and itinerary costs. Let students interview working adults to determine the literacy demands of given jobs. Have them write a letter to the editor or an article on this for a newspaper.

Use Real-World Reading in Content Areas. You know how some teachers are very clever at creating real-world reading and writing tasks to fit their content area subjects. Here are some examples of materials and activities for specific content areas suggested by Mikulecky (1989).

Social Studies

Maps	Newspapers	Bank Statements	Atlas
Magazines	Travel Pamphlets	Charts-Graphs	Voting Rules
Contracts	Tax Forms	Family Tree	Stock Reports

- *Use the materials to plan trips, write reports and letters.*
- *Interview parents and adults with experience in travel or history. Videotape and write a summary (an oral history) report.*

Science

Pamphlets	Medicine Instructions	Newspapers	Catalogs
Farm Journals	Lab Procedures	Weather Data	Labels

- *Study chemicals added to foods.*
- *Interpret medical records and terms.*
- *Arrange student teams to monitor news on space, weather, medicine.*

- *Have students study computer applications to school communication and student-computer-use needs.*
- *Use garden and seed catalogs to study how to improve the local environment.*

Mathematics

Pricing from Ads   Tax Forms   Bank Accounts   Interest Tables
Used Car Guides   Recipes   Newspapers   Financial Aid Forms
Supermarket and restaurant receipts   Mileage Maps

- *Alter a recipe for larger or smaller servings.*
- *Compare prices of used cars and include loan interest costs.*
- *Copy a monthly bank statement and use the data to write a profile of how the money was spent.*
- *Convert graphic data into paragraphs and paragraph information into graphs and charts.*

Industrial Arts

Blueprints   Computer Manuals   Parts Manuals
Service Manuals   Construction Contracts   Estimates
Owner Manuals   Schematic Drawings   Trade Journals

- *Dismantle and rebuild a carburetor using the instructions from a kit.*
- *Diagnose a broken lawn mower using a service manual.*
- *Have students do the paperwork for the repair of a car or appliance.*

These are only a few of the ways you can use materials from the community to model out-of-school reading and writing. In this way you'll bring the students and community closer together as literacy tasks are viewed in the meaningful context of the adult world of work. Another good reason to use out-of-school materials is the simple fact that the ability to comprehend school-oriented stories and good literature does not transfer very well to reading repair manuals, tax forms, and assembly instructions (Mikulecky, 1989, p. 130). In fact Sticht (1986) suggests that job experience and use of work-related print materials might account for as much as three to four grade levels in job reading ability over tested school reading levels.

In addition to using real-world literacy materials for reading and writing assignments, schools in Michigan are closing the gap between schools and the community with student employability portfolios.

Employability Portfolios

One way parents and businesses are more involved with schools in Michigan is through the use of the Employability Skills Portfolio (ESP). Students in grades 6 to 12 develop portfolios (Stemmer, et al., 1992) that contain evidence about their academic strengths, personal management performance, and teamwork abilities. The purpose of preparing this evidence was not to compete to see who was employable for a specific job. The idea was that because today's students will change careers several times in a lifetime, it is important to know how to document one's growth. The portfolio is a way to document answers to the question "Can you do the job?"

Portfolios are organized around the general skills that students need, not only at an entry-level but at jobs of all levels. Here is a prototype skills profile:

Academic Skills

- Read and understand written materials
- Understand charts and graphs
- Understand basic math
- Use math to solve problems
- Use research and library skills
- Use specialized knowledge and skills to complete a job
- Use tools and equipment
- Speak the language in which business is conducted
- Write the language in which business is conducted
- Use scientific method to solve problems

Personal Management Skills

- Attend school/work daily and on time
- Meet school/work deadlines
- Develop career plans
- Know personal strengths and weaknesses
- Demonstrate self-control
- Pay attention to details
- Follow written and oral instructions/directions
- Work without supervision
- Learn new skills
- Identify and suggest better ways to get the job done

Teamwork Skills

- Actively participate in group
- Know group's rules and values

- Listen to other group members
- Express ideas to other members
- Be sensitive to other members' views and ideas
- Be willing to compromise in order to best accomplish goals
- Be a leader or a follower to best accomplish goals
- Work in changing settings and with people of different backgrounds

The portfolios are used in several ways to create a valuable school-community collaboration that places literacy in a practical and natural workplace context. Parents are involved in helping students complete portfolios, and local businesses review the materials and give feedback to individual students. Employers are invited to school for mock interviews, and after reviewing portfolios, they inform students of their qualifications for specific jobs. Employers also give students ideas about how to improve and document their skills. The portfolios also lead students to interview employers and workers in their community offices and other job sites. After these interviews, students report back to fellow students and share tips for improving job-related literacy skills.

The Michigan experience indicated that portfolios were a way to increase involvement between teachers, parents, and businesses. A particularly effective outcome was a guide that showed parents how to motivate children to improve employability. Parents also came to school to participate in interviews, make class presentations about their work, and write letters of support for the use of portfolios. Businesses participated by providing pilot sites for presentations, interviews, field trips, and opportunities for students to "shadow" adults at work on a one-to-one basis. Some communities even created a business advisory group to work with the schools.

The schools reported that an efficient way to introduce portfolios was to have teachers who had all of the students, such as a middle-grade or junior high English teacher, use them in class. In English, reading, and language arts classes, student essays and papers on career topics were placed in the portfolios. Other materials placed in the portfolios included awards, test results, performance appraisals from teachers, transcripts, descriptions and grades for career-related projects, and even letters from employers. Cooperative learning records and materials were also used as evidence of teamwork skills.

Portfolios were often kept in files at the school, although storage and security were not problems when students maintained their own records. Teachers also reported that when students kept their own records it was a challenge to help them understand how to decide what to keep and what to omit.

Although personal portfolios have the potential to show students how literacy applies to careers and work, some schools go further. In Indiana, teachers, principals, and parents let students operate a student-run school book store or school supply store.

Student-Operated Bookshops

Another way that schools and businesses work together to encourage literacy is to establish student-managed paperback bookshops (Braught, 1992). With this approach, middle-grade students, teachers, administrators, parents, and local businesses combine their efforts to establish an "ongoing book fair of discounted paperbacks, managed entirely by students as a regular school activity" (Braught, p. 439). Start-up efforts often involve a teacher going to a community service agency or a group of businesses for initial funds ($500) to establish a workable program. There were initial concerns that local vendors would resent competition from low-overhead school bookshops. However, many book vendors said that, because middle-grade students are not their regular customers, they wanted to encourage any effort to expand this market.

Bookshops are usually operated by students under the direction of a board of directors. The board usually includes a small number of teachers, parents and/or community business persons, and about 20 students. The leadership of the board is a student responsibility, and the student members have to be reliable workers who can work together.

The practical experiences of operating a bookshop erase typical gaps between school literacy and workplace literacy. For example, students learn to work with distributors who meet the following pricing and distributing criteria (Braught, p. 443):

1. *A 40% discount on orders of 50 or fewer books.*
2. *A current free catalog with a large and interesting inventory.*
3. *Shipping and handling costs of no more than 2% of the total order.*
4. *Delivery of books within 2 weeks of an order.*
5. *Toll-free telephone ordering and cordial representatives.*
6. *Special services that eliminate back ordering, offer occasional special offers, and accept returns of damaged or unsold books with full credit.*

Experienced bookshop leaders recommend the following distributors who meet these criteria: (Source is Braught, 1992, p. 443)

- Ingram Library Services, 1125 Heil Quaker Blvd., Laverne, Tenn. 37086, 800-937-8000 (Requires 100+ titles for a 40% discount)

- Mr. Paperback, 2914 Independence Dr., Ft. Wayne, Ind. 46808, 800-525-7204 (Small inventory, but dependable)
- NACSCORP, 528 E. Lorain St., Oberlin, Ohio 44074-1298, 800-622-7498 (Meets criteria, requires $100 membership)
- Scholastic/Readers Choice, P.O. Box 7501, Jefferson City, Mo. 65102, 800-325-614 (Area reps used who may not have a toll-free number)
- The Bookmen, 525 N. 3rd St., Minneapolis, Minn. 55401, 800-328-8411 (Popular with bookshops for meeting criteria)

The bookshop idea is one way to provide a natural and practical literacy connection between schools and the local community. More information based on over 60 bookshop projects is available by writing: School Bookshops Project, SE 710, Indiana State University, Terre Haute, Ind. 47809, phone 812-237-2836.

Summary

This chapter contained ideas for connecting teachers, parents, and the community to provide literacy learning that is natural, pleasurable, and practical. The intent was to move away from a strict "in-school" view of literacy to embrace a broader community-accountability idea. Ideas for accomplishing this included: treating parents as coequals rather than as clients; celebrating literacy practices; and tapping community talent. Another intent was a reminder that we should not expect artistic works of literature to be the only literacy material teachers use. Ideas for involving businesses and the world of work included: selecting and using a wide variety of materials from the world of work; using student employability portfolios; and the establishment of student-operated bookstores.

Ideas for approaching literacy from a broad community perspective are endless, and teachers and principals are very creative as they "vision" how to make literacy learning meaningful. This chapter touched on just a few of the ideas that exist today. The next chapter examines school improvement funding from a teacher's viewpoint and describes several ways that teachers are changing the way schools pay for literacy learning.

References

Bloome, D. (1985). Reading as a social process. *Language Arts, 62,* 134–142.

Braught, L. R. (1992). Student operated paperback bookshops: A program to encourage middle-grade literacy. *The Reading Teacher, 45,* 438–444.

Davis, B. C. (October 1989). A successful parent involvement program, *Educational Leadership, 47*(2), 21–23.

Griffin, W. M. (May 1988). Read aloud week at Collicot school. *Educational Leadership, 45*(9), 57.

Hunter, M. (October 1989). Join the "Par-aide" in education. *Educational Leadership, 47*(2), 36–41.

Lingle, J. C. (October 1989). What do parents want from principals and teachers? *Educational Leadership, 47*(2), 12–14.

Losen, S., and Diament, B. (1978). *Parent conferences in the schools: Procedures for developing effective partnerships.* Boston: Allyn and Bacon.

Mikulecky, L. (1989). Real-world literacy demands: How they've changed and what teachers can do. In Lapp, D., Flood, J., and Farnan, N. (Eds.). *Content area reading and learning: Instructional strategies.* Englewood Cliffs, N.J.: Prentice Hall, 123–136.

Mikulecky, L. (1991). National adult literacy and lifelong learning goals. *Phi Delta Kappan, 72,* 304–309.

Piazza, C. L., and Tomlinson, C. M. (1985). A concert of writers. *Language Arts, 62,* 150–158.

Seeley, D. S. (October 1989). A new paradigm for parent involvement. *Educational Leadership, 47*(2), 46–48.

Stemmer, P., Brown, B., and Smith, C. (March 1992). The employability skills portfolio. *Educational Leadership, 49*(7), 32–35.

Sticht, T. G., et al. (1986). *Teachers, books, computers, and peers: Integrated communications technologies for adult literacy development.* Monterey, Calif.: U.S. Naval Postgraduate School.

9

Changing School Funding Practices

*Two decades, three school districts, and seven school buildings into my teaching career I am still spending money from my personal income on my elementary class.**

In this chapter I will describe how teachers are changing the way literacy programs are funded. I will also explain how you might go about changing your own spending patterns, your school spending practices, and even your district school improvement financial policies.

To start this discussion let us look at the practice of spending our own money to do our job. Tour the Yellow Pages in your phone book and you will probably find a business called "Teacher Supply Store" where you can buy a wide variety of classroom materials. Attend a teacher conference and there will be an exhibition hall where you can buy everything from balls to books, rulers to rubber stamps, and paper to puppets. As a teacher you spend your own money on teaching supplies. In this chapter I want you to first consider why teachers continue to do this. Later in the chapter we will consider other funding issues, and what they suggest about the financing of school improvement. But for now we will examine our own personal spending.

I recall how, over 20 years ago, special education teachers whose rooms had been moved to our school were talking about where they

---

*Linda Moore, 1992. *Picking Up the Slack: Teachers Subsidizing the System,* p. 1.

could buy yellow chalk. As a new principal I interrupted to tell them we had plenty on hand in our storeroom and that our secretary, Alma, had developed an efficient system through which teachers could easily get a wide variety of teaching supplies. They were pleased when they were able to order what they needed. I was surprised to learn the extent to which they were spending their own money for paper, pencils, and a whole host of items that the district had already purchased for them. They told me that special education teachers often had to "go around" the local principal and send their requests to the central office special education administrators. And because this took a long time and often became fouled up, it was easier to buy what they needed themselves.

Today, teachers continue to quietly subsidize schools by buying books, supplies, and equipment with their own money. Latham and Fifield (1993) surveyed 360 teachers in two western states, and 81 percent reported that the average annual amount spent was $511 for elementary teachers, $289 for middle/junior high teachers, and $484 for high school teachers.

In a recent small-scale study (Moore, 1992), 20 teachers kept track of school-related spending from June through October. In these five months they subsidized their classrooms by a total of $7,725. The top three categories were books ($2,375), supplies ($1,462), and equipment ($1,083). The range of spending was a substantial one-hundred-fold. One teacher reported spending $17 over the five months while another reported a total of $1,761! The median was $171 and the mean was $386. Four special-education teachers averaged $557 each, outspending 12 regular classroom teachers who averaged $344. Moore estimated that if the averages from these 20 teachers were projected over an entire year the total would approximate $18,540, or more than $900 per teacher. She says this "amount of money . . . is substantial and constitutes an unseen grant provided to school districts on a yearly basis—no questions asked; no forms to fill out" (p. 36).

To better understand personal spending, Moore asked them to check any of several statements that applied to their own situation. Seventeen of the 20 teachers (85 percent) said the amount budgeted by the district is inadequate. Twelve (60 percent) said the purchase order routine takes too long and some of the things they need cannot be obtained with a purchase order. Eleven (55 percent) said they need innovative materials throughout the year and one large order in the spring is too restrictive. Ten (50 percent) said their district was experiencing financial difficulties; they could obtain supplies cheaper on their own; and they had changed their teaching so that existing materials were no longer adequate. The least frequently checked items were: the administrator does not let me use the revolving funds (six or 30 percent); and the reimbursement procedures in the district are too much of a hassle (four or 20 percent).

Perhaps these are some of the workplace reasons that also lead you to spend your own money. But there are also very powerful personal or internal reasons that drive teachers to use personal money. Teaching is very personal, and in order to create a learning environment that reflects a personal vision or image of learning, teachers take some action to make this vision a reality (Johnston, 1990). So when you see and feel a gap between your personal image of learning and teaching and what your school provides, your vision is powerful enough to drive you to spend your own money on books, materials, and equipment.

In this chapter I want you to question personal spending and consider other alternatives for obtaining books, materials, and equipment that match your vision of classroom teaching and learning. Moore (1992) said that after 20 years she was seriously questioning using her personal income to subsidize the school. I am suggesting that there is something fundamentally wrong when children might get access to new and better books, materials, and equipment simply because their teacher can afford it. Remember how one of the 20 teachers in Moore's study reported spending a total of $17 while another spent $1,700? Of course, we do not know if the teacher who spent the least had greater access to grants or other school money than the one who spent the most. But we suspect otherwise. And we certainly should not accept the idea that some students have a "poorer" teacher who has one hundred times less the purchasing power of another.

I have one caution about personal spending: I don't want you to stop buying personal books with your own money. I'm not urging you to rely on funds from others to buy professional books you wish to read personally. As true professionals, we ought to spend our own money on books we choose to read. After all, if we are truly *real* readers we will spend our own money on our own books.

The information and ideas in this chapter provide alternatives that you can use to grow from being a "dedicated" teacher, who buys instructional materials with your own money, to a "professional" teacher, who joins with others to influence boards and administrators to allocate adequate funds and provide adequate teaching materials for all teachers (McHenry, 1989). One important alternative is to work with other teachers to influence the policymakers at the local level to spend school improvement money in new ways. For example, instead of paying only consultants, curriculum specialists, and other top-down change agents, why not do like some districts and pay classroom teachers and principals for implementing changes? In the next section we will examine current financial patterns and suggest several guidelines for funding grass-roots efforts to improve school literacy programs.

The Big Picture of School Improvement Funding

Owing mainly to school accounting procedures (Kirst, 1988; Odden and Picus, 1992), it is difficult to determine specific amounts spent on new teaching materials, school improvement, curriculum change, and other school improvement activities. California is one of the few states that have data sources that school finance experts can study. And even these data are very general. For example, statewide California data from the mid-1980s reveal that districts spend around 5 percent of their total school dollars on books, supplies, and equipment and about 2 percent on school improvement (Kirst, 1988, pp. 374–386). California data indicate that, for the most part, local school improvement funds are spent, first, on district specialists who plan and lead school improvement activities, and second, on substitute teachers who cover classes while teachers are away. But the largest investment in school improvement that accrues are the salary advances that teachers receive as a "result of advanced university course work or salary credits awarded by the district" (Kirst, 1988, p. 385). Does this investment pay off? School improvement studies in California (Kirst, 1988, pp. 385–386) revealed that there is a financial commitment to improving teacher knowledge and practice, and that local district capacity to deliver school improvement has improved. However, the payoff news is not good. Researchers concluded that current California school improvement activities and incentives appear unlikely to yield substantial change in classroom teacher thinking or performance. Reasons for this included the finding that funds are spent to reinforce existing conventional structures and long-standing traditions in teaching, and that school improvement is relatively unevaluated in comparison with other educational initiatives. Overall, this California study concluded that, while funds are appropriated for school improvement, there is no comprehensive or consistent school improvement policy to guide institutional decision making and accountability.

These findings raise serious policy questions. Why should districts pay you to complete university courses that not only may be unrelated to district priorities, but also may not result in improved classroom teaching? Why pay curriculum specialist salaries and consultant fees in the absence of accountability for changes in classroom instruction and improved schooling? Kirst (1988, p. 388) concluded that it is unlikely that those of us who are "professional educators" will lead the search for answers to these questions because we are "comfortable" with the existing fiscal information system. He asserts that pressure for better account-ability for school improvement spending will have to come from elected officials, the media, and the business community.

From your perspective as a teacher, do you agree with this? Is there adequate support in your district for teaching materials and school improvement? Do incentives like salary increases for taking graduate classes lead to actual changes and improvements in your classroom effectiveness? Does money spent in your district on curriculum specialist salaries and consultants lead to improving your effectiveness in the classroom? Teachers and principals who are not satisfied with current financial policies have reason to be concerned. Financial studies indicate that restructured schools spend one-half of one percent on school im-provement while restructured corporations spend 15 to 20 percent of their revenue on similar activities (Fiske, 1991, p. 254). We all ought to be very concerned about the amount and control of money for acquiring promising new teaching materials, supplies, and equipment. We all ought to wonder if some of the money spent on curriculum-specialist salaries and consultant fees wouldn't be better directed into teachers pockets as incentives for implementing changes. If you are not comfort-able with all of the current financial arrangements, you may want to consider bringing pressure from within, from the grass roots, to see that money is spent in ways that lead directly to improved literacy learning.

Redirecting Local School Improvement Financing

Many school improvement funds are spent on experts who, like appli-ance servicemen, are supposed to supply quick fixes. To rethink how we spend school improvement money, consider the following scenario. As the school improvement session on writing across the curriculum was ending, it occurred to Mike that the real beneficiary from the meeting was the consultant who pocketed a $500 fee for the day's work. Even though the presentation and activities were so-so and the speaker was eloquent, the ideas were not all directed at the real literacy concerns Mike faced in his seventh-grade classroom. As he reflected on the consultant's work, it was obvious that some sweeping changes in how his school district financed school improvement were needed. It occurred to Mike that nothing would change unless he implemented changes in his own classroom. But what would it take to motivate him to do it? While the consultant was motivated to lead a teacher training session by a $500 fee, what incentive was there for Mike to make the effort to introduce some new writing ideas into his social studies class?

What incentive is there for you? Does your school district have a top-down school finance plan in which school improvement money is mainly used by consultants and specialists? Such a plan means that change is viewed as a top down event that only occurs when pressure is applied from outside the school. If you want change to occur from inside the school, here are five ideas that schools are implementing to make sure that more of the money for change is invested where it should be—on helping the local staff grow. For teachers, a reasonable goal is to work with other teachers and administrators to seek funds that are both local and long term. To do this teachers are using their political power to negotiate the following policies and practices:

Keep the Money Close to the Classroom

Bracey (1991) reported that after 25 years of trying to change education we know that what happens at the smallest unit (the school, the class-room, the individual teacher) is the most important. Instead of spending most of the money on big-name visitors, some districts, such as Wheeling, Ill. (1987), use a good portion of their school improvement money to support teachers, principals, and others who are close to the students. An 80/20 split between money spent on staff members and money spent on visiting firemen is about right (Erickson, 1987). To encourage individuals who want to implement new ideas, some districts send teachers to workshops and courses. Other schools designate money for materials so that teachers who are trying to change their teaching can get what they need. Another idea that works is to hire consultants that principals and teachers ask for, and they come only at a time that is convenient for the staff.

Some school boards and teacher unions cooperate to establish improvement funds. Rewards and incentives are given to teachers and principals who implement changes. These funds are usually handled like local grants that are directed by a committee representing the teachers and the school board. Other schools offer stipends for travel to visit other schools, summer work arrangements for curriculum development, and direct payments of $100 (negotiable) per hour for local teachers who direct local workshops. One unique idea is to adopt a sales business strategy. Teachers who implement changes earn "points" that apply to vouchers for personal (and professional) airline and lodging travel arrangements.

Fund a Local Cadre

Many schools use consultants to help set up school improvement cadres consisting of local teachers, principals, and parents. Having a local cadre of change agents ensures that resident experts will be available when the visiting fireman have left. Cadres work in varying ways, but they typically serve as advocates for planned change (Howey and Vaughn, 1983). This is important, given the resistance of schools to the inherent messiness of change. The problem is that schools are arranged to run efficiently, and since change threatens efficiency, cadres are useful because they can protect initial attempts to change the status quo. Cadres can also protect long-term change activities. Establishing a local cadre is smart, because no single group in a school system or community has enough power to mandate and implement important changes. Involving parents, businesspeople, and other nonschool people from the community broadens the power base. This increases the chances of protecting change activities for a long enough time for them to become part of the norm. When budgeting for school improvement, try to figure on spending about half of the 20 percent allotted to consultants on funding a local cadre of change agents.

Fund "Learning Communities"

A powerful concept that schools find useful for improving learning is to have small groups of teachers meet regularly to share ideas and support each other as they grow. Learning communities (Dodd and Rosenbaum, 1986; Glickman, 1992) are often more potent, and less expensive, than meetings featuring outside experts. Teachers determine the form and direction of their "learning" and meet more frequently to discuss specific ideas that fit their working conditions. Groups of teachers who are successful at sharing and planning changes often become very enthusiastic and even meet on their own time. Budgeting money for materials, travel, refreshments, and other means of supporting local learning communities is money well spent.

Don't Waste Funds on Too Many Small-scale Reforms

Although it is tempting, stretching limited school improvement dollars over many small-scale improvement efforts may result in negligible effects. A "one problem/one solution approach (Bracey, p. 557)" ignores the fact that school issues are all related parts of a larger system. Aiming change efforts at discrete or narrow aspects of school systems is likely to fail. Real improvement usually involves fundamental changes in roles, policies, materials, reward systems, and certainly classroom practices. Real improvement requires the cooperative efforts of teachers, principals, parents, consultants, and administrators—and money. Instead of many little projects, budget for a few long-term school improvement efforts that will have some significant payoff. For example, it will take from three to six years to make significant changes in moving away from typical rigid classroom grouping to flexible grouping, or from a standardized testing accountability system to one featuring more teacher observation and student portfolios.

On the other hand, many school watchers and other constituents will be looking for some speedy results. So it's wise to set aside some money for one or two quick-fix improvement projects to let taxpayers know the school system is moving ahead. A single effort, like buying good children's literature books and publicizing their use, is a good example of this. But true and lasting improvements will come when long term money is invested in long-term change activities.

Avoid Wasting Money on an Import Syndrome or a List Mentality

A common mistake is to spend large amounts of money trying to copy another school system's curriculum, materials, methods, or organizational plans for reading and writing. It's also common to try to implement a list of practices or characteristics from another system. The fault of both of these is that, while other people's practices are good starting points, your own plan must be based on the character and goals of your own school or district. A sure way to waste money is to blindly import ideas from others, regardless of how well they worked there, or simply follow lists provided by state agencies or eminent scholars.

Barth (1986) accurately points out that there are two sources of knowledge for improving learning in schools. One is research (logical lists of effective practices), and the other is the "craft knowledge of school people" (p. 296). Lists of effective practices are useful for helping teachers and principals clarify their own visions of the way they want their schools and classrooms to operate. Used in this way, lists can be a useful starting point. When teachers and principals look at the lists and see that they are already doing some good things, they are motivated to move ahead, and the most important "answers or solutions that are reached will come from within" (p. 296).

The focus of school improvement financing is right when most of the money "stays home"—as incentives and support for staff members who work in the local school every day. True improvement is best characterized as growth. And growth depends upon changes made by classroom teachers and principals who are with the students every day. In order to fund growth it is necessary to have fiscal policies that ensure that curriculum and school improvement money comes in sustained contact with the grass roots.

Seeking External Funding for Literacy Improvement

One way you, as a professional teacher, can move beyond being "dedicated" and spending your own money is to obtain support from a grant source. Grants are basically a financial support agreement between you (the project leader or principal investigator) and a sponsor who thinks your idea has merit. There are many types of awards. In addition to the typical basic or applied research grants that support theory and hypotheses testing, there are *teacher-as-researcher grants* that support studies conducted in schools and classrooms. Usually teacher-as-researcher grants support efforts to examine the effects of instructional-oriented teaching methods. *Demonstration grants* are another source of support for illustrating the effectiveness of a promising school practice. There are also *training grants* to support the cost of specific training in teaching skills, as well as *material and equipment grants* to help schools improve. Sometimes *planning grants* are awarded to schools to support new and future improvement efforts.

Grass-Roots Grant Sources

A first step in seeking a grant for improving literacy learning is to identify agencies that might be interested in sponsoring your program. It is important to have up-to-date knowledge of possible funding sources. One source is a local university that may have a special office that coordinates grant seeking. It will have a resource library with current information about funding sources. Other sources are state and regional educational service centers that coordinate and provide services to school districts in their area. And do not overlook your local board of education and administrative office. Very often they have lists of current sources that you can direct your inquiries to about possible funding.

Other promising sources are state and national professional associations. For example, in Illinois the Illinois Reading Council will award small financial grants to local reading councils. Awards are given for activities that promote literacy development in school and community, and professional development opportunities that lead to improved instruction in reading and writing. These local awards are usually limited to $500, and applications are due in February of each year. Detailed information is available from Chair, Grants Committee, Illinois Reading Council, P.O. Box 367, Bloomington, Ill. 61702-0367 (309-662-5093).

The International Reading Association also awards grants up to $5,000 to support promising reading research. Proposals are usually due in December, and awards do not support new programs or instructional materials, except when these expenditures are necessary for conducting research. More information is available from Elva Knight Research Grants, International Reading Association, 800 Barksdale Road, P.O. Box 8139, Newark, Del. 19714-8139 (302-731-1600).

The National Council of Teachers of English awards teacher-researcher and collaboration grants. The teacher-researcher grants have a limit of $1,500 and are designed to support classroom-based research. Examples of funded studies include Better than Basals: A Teacher-Developed Literature Program, and Children's Use of Punctuation: A Follow-Up Study. Collaboration grants support cooperative research conducted by teachers and university researchers. These grants have a limit of $5,000 and cannot fund degree-related research. Proposals are usually due by mid-February, and applications are available from Project Assistant , NCTE Research Foundation, 1111 Kenyon Road, Urbana, Ill. 61801 (217-328-3870).

Other local sources of funding for literacy improvement are parent-teacher organizations and community service agencies. Very often these groups welcome the chance to support their local schools by funding well-thought-out projects. Local groups are excellent sources of funds, especially for materials (books, magazines, and other media) and equipment (book binding, personal computers, television, camcorders, and other audio-visual) that support literacy activities. The trick is to think, write a plan, and ask. In the next section you will read about how to plan and write a funding proposal.

Grant Proposal Writing

Another step in seeking funds to improve literacy learning is to invest in a good reference book on grant writing, such as David R. Krathwohl's *How to Prepare a Research Proposal* (2nd ed.), Syracuse University Bookstore, 303 University Place, Syracuse, N.Y. 13210. This book, as well as others, will provide important information to guide your thinking and help you avoid mistakes. To increase your chances of obtaining funds, you should pay attention to what successful grant seekers have to say about pre-planning and writing. For example, here are some key preplanning tasks:

• Review the literature, gather data, and assess other studies and projects that address your proposal. This will help later at the writing stage, because you can define your approach better and describe its importance and potential contribution.

- Think about your degree of training and experience. This will help determine whether you need to solicit the help of a more experienced teacher-researcher. This is also the time to build support and involvement of others in the project.
- Consider the funding need and the level of support you need to do the project. Money has a way of defining methods and even objectives. Check carefully with possible funding agencies as to what they will and will not pay for.
- Determine the level of financial support and time commitment that is available from your school. Can you get released time? Does the proposed sponsor require that your school donate certain resources such as clerical help or use of equipment?
- Contact a person at the proposed funding source either by letter or telephone. Some agencies require a letter of inquiry even before a proposal is at the writing stage.
- Before you begin writing, request and review application guidelines from the sponsoring agency. These guidelines will tell you whether your project is eligible. They will also describe the length and format that you must follow. It is crucial to adhere to these guidelines in order to even be considered for funding.

When you get to the writing stage, it is a good idea to not use a committee. The fewer the writers the better. You should visualize your audience as one person. Write in the third person, because it is easier to praise "them" than "me." You should write clearly in the active voice, keeping your paragraphs short and limited to one concept. Try to keep sentences to 15 words or less, with no more than two commas. Start off with the important points, catch the reader's attention early, and accentuate the positive with words like "opportunities" and "growth" rather than "needs." Beware of jargon, vague references, and abbreviations. It is better to communicate clearly than it is to try to impress the readers. They are sophisticated and experienced and there is no need to be sly, cute, or overdramatic. You should be prepared to complete the following typical sections:

1. A *title page/cover sheet* is usually supplied by the the agency. Select an appropriate and interesting title of ten words or less.
2. A brief and accurate *abstract/summary* of 100 to 500 words is a very important section. It describes the need, objectives, activities, outcomes, and dissemination plans of the project.

3. A statement of *the problem or need* will tell why the project will make a contribution, cover new ground, and build on previous work. This section contains the literature review in which you demonstrate your familiarity with the related research and show how the projects fits in. Sometimes statistical or demographic data are needed in this section to support the problem.

4. A section of *goals and objectives* identifies outcomes and what the project is to achieve. Goals are more general descriptions of the ideal outcomes. Objectives tell how you plan to reach the goals. They must be specific, measurable statements that are compatible with the project goals.

5. The section on *procedures/methodology* is the heart of the proposal. Here is where you provide a chronological list of details to tell exactly how you plan to proceed. What services will be provided? How will training be accomplished? Who are the participants? What materials will be used? What is the time frame and what data will be generated? How will the data be analyzed and reported? Have this part reread and edited to make sure it clearly states what you intend to do.

6. You will also need to describe the *personnel* involved in the project in terms of their qualifications, selection, duties, time of involvement, and relationships with each other and the project leaders. If consultants are used you will need to justify their involvement and relate their credentials and qualifications to the project goals and objectives.

7. In this part you will tell how the *project outcomes* will be evaluated. How will the project staff know when and if the goals and objectives have been met? What data will be collected, how will it be gathered and analyzed? Proposals often must describe how ongoing (formative) evaluation may lead to modifications in the project, as well as how a final (summative) evaluation will be conducted.

8. Very often a grant has a section on *dissemination and continuation* that tells how the results might be shared. This might include plans for a report, a journal article, a paper at a professional meeting, or even a manual or handbook. Many granting agencies would like the project to extend beyond the grant funding period. Some proposals require that you describe how your school will assume financial and/or programmatic responsibility after the grant time period.

9. A very important part of the grant is the *budget*. Advanced planning with someone in the proposed granting agency or someone familiar with grant budgets is necessary to avoid rejection (the worst case) or the need for last-minute revisions (the usual case). Budgets describe cost over time for: salaries and wages, fringe benefits, equipment, travel, materials and supplies, and other costs such as photocopying, postage, telephone, or consultant fees. Very often this section contains a budget justification section that explains the reasons for each of the items in the budget. It is advisable to have an experienced budget or school finance specialist review the budget well in advance of the agency deadline.

Completing all of these writing tasks is a lot of work. But the writing itself is often beneficial. You will be better able to justify and defend your teaching practices. You may encounter new ideas that you can incorporate into your existing program. You will sharpen your planning skills and perhaps you will even be able to see how to improve your literacy program even if your grant proposal is turned down. This possibility is important to consider. If you are rejected you should ask to see the reviews of your project. Finally, you should consider the possibility of rewriting and resubmitting. Successful grant seekers agree that a key to success is perseverance.

Example of Teacher-Developed Literacy Improvement Grant

Evelyn Bailey and Linda Hileman, teachers in Jonesboro, Illinois, District 43, were awarded a School Improvement Change Grant from the Illinois State Board of Education in December 1992. These teachers asked for and received $10,000 to implement whole-language approaches to reading and writing in their K-8 school. A description of their grant is shown in Box 9-1.

Summary

Influencing your local district policies and writing grants are two ways you can move from being dedicated (spending your own money) to being professional. This chapter presented data on how much of their own money some teachers spend, and a discussion of school finance as it relates to school improvement. The picture that emerges from this information is that current school improvement financing practices fall short of the mark. The amount spent is barely enough and there is a lack of accountability. A basic problem is that money that is available is spent on outside or top-down change processes. Guidelines for changing local funding policies and practices were presented to show how financial responsibilities and incentives are being directed at the grass-roots level. Finally, several grant sources and tips for grant writing were presented to show how teachers can obtain support for improving literacy learning.

BOX 9-1   Sample Grant

Abstract

The focus of this grant is to plan for the creation of a climate conducive to change in the language arts program in Jonesboro Public School District 43. The grant has two purposes: (1) Teachers will identify and develop support systems within the school building, the community, and region. These support systems will involve: School District 43 staff members, parents and other community members, community resource persons, personnel at other area schools, and language arts consultants; (2) teachers and aides will identify current and additional resources needed to integrate the current curriculum with the language arts curriculum recommended in the local assessment plan and Illinois Learning Outcome Goals 4, 5, and 6.

It is expected that, through this grant, improvement in the attitude of teachers, parents, and students toward the language arts will occur, and in turn, student achievement will rise. In addition, staff relations will improve through collaboration and cooperation.

Narrative

Jonesboro, Illinois is a rural community in Union County, located approximately 120 miles southeast of St. Louis, Missouri. School District 43, with a K-8 enrollment of 430 students, receives about 82 percent of its funding from State and Federal sources. The district is currently experiencing diminished financial resources and must rely on the creativity and determination of the local staff to maintain and improve educational opportunities.

The district has piloted the new Iowa Test of Basic Skills in all grades and has purchased the Houghton-Mifflin Literature program. This step was the beginning of an attempt to improve the language arts curriculum and implement a whole-language approach to reading and writing.

However, materials alone cannot bring about the needed changes. Schools are organized to "run," not change. Because of scheduling, teachers are isolated from each other. Because the new materials are unfamiliar and some of the whole-language teaching processes are new, teachers feel overwhelmed and discouraged. Misunderstandings occur when teachers try to explain their frustrations.

This grant will give each language arts teacher in grades K-8 opportunities to meet weekly after school with their partner teacher at the same grade level, with the teachers of grades before and after their level, and/or with the library staff. Through these meetings the philosophy and practices of whole-language at Jonesboro School will be constantly reviewed and revised as teachers gain new insights and identify and coordinate available resources.

The grant will also encourage and enable teachers to receive information and training by working with consultants, by attending conferences, and by visiting other whole-language classrooms in the area. It will also allow the school to increase parent communication, to better inform, gain support, and discover new community resources that support instructional themes and units of study.

By creating this atmosphere of support for change within the school, within the small town, and within the educational community of the region, teachers will be informed, empowered, and enthused. This will not only promote enjoyment of literature and improve student achievement in the language arts, but will also lead to systematic change through staff collaboration and cooperation. The completion of this project should also provide an excellent template for other school districts as they prepare to systematically approach school improvement in the language arts.

Evaluation

The evaluation process will use data from teacher questionnaires administered from January to August. The questionnaires will examine changes in teachers' attitudes and behaviors related to whole-language teaching as well as changes in students' attitudes and behaviors. See Appendix A for a copy of the evaluation forms.

In addition, the coordinators will conduct monthly formative evaluations through information gained during the after-school meetings.

Finally, a descriptive outline should be in place by the end of the project. This document will clearly outline the planning process for impacting curriculum change in language arts for the entire K-8 school district.

Activities, Time Line, Resources, and Budget

Activity I: Teacher Collaboration

Time:	January through August 1993
Description:	Language arts teachers will meet weekly, after school, for at least one hour to collaborate and cooperatively discuss the implementation of whole-language methods and materials.
Responsibility:	The grant coordinators will organize these meetings and keep records of discussions, plans, and decisions.
Cost:	Stipends for 16 teachers @ $10 per hour for 32 sessions = $5,120

Activity II: Library Aide

Time:	January through August 1993
Description:	The current library aide will extend her work day by one hour, in order to assist classroom teachers in coordinat-

Continued

BOX 9-1   *Continued*

	ing existing library resources with the new whole-language themes.
Responsibility:	The grant coordinators will administer the time sheet and assignment recordkeeping.
Cost:	Salary of library aide: 120 hours @ $6.20 = $744

Activity III: Consultation with Houghton-Mifflin Textbook Representative

Time Line:	Dates to be determined between January-August 1993
Description:	Substitutes will be hired to release teachers to meet with text consultant, who is available at no cost to the district.
Responsibility:	Grant coordinators will arrange meeting times.
Cost:	Two days of substitute pay @ $50 per day = $100

Activity IV: Workshops and Conferences

Time Line:	January through August 1993
Description:	Teachers will attend regional or state sessions related to whole-language approaches to reading and writing instruction.
Responsibility:	Grant coordinators will make all arrangements.

Cost:

Substitute pay for 12 days of released time @ $50 per day:	$600
Registration Fees:	$300
Lodging, meals, transportation @ $.26 per mile:	$553
Total:	$1,453

Activity V: On-site Classroom Visitation

Time Line:	January through June 1993
Description:	Teachers will receive released time to observe other teachers and schools successfully implementing whole-language methods.
Responsibility:	Grant coordinators will make all arrangements.

BOX 9-1 *Continued*

Cost:	Substitute pay for 12 days of teacher released time @ $50 per day:	$600
	Lodging, meals, transportation @ $.26 per mile:	$553
	Total:	$1,153
	Total cost of all five activities:	$8,570
	General Administration Cost of secretary, bookkeeping, program arrangements @ $10 per hour for 143 hours:	$1,430
Total Grant Amount		$10,000

References

Barth, R. S. (1986). On sheep and goats and school reform. *Phi Delta Kappan, 68,* 293–296.

Bracey, G. W. (1991). Educational change. *Phi Delta Kappan, 72,* 557–560.

Dodd, A., and Rosenbaum, E. (1986). Learning communities for curriculum and school improvement. *Phi Delta Kappan, 67,* 380–384.

Erickson, L. G. (1987). School improvement: Five ways to keep things in focus. *The Executive Educator, 9,* 24.

Fiske, E. B. (1991). *Smart schools, smart kids: Why do some schools work?* New York: Simon and Schuster.

Glickman, C. D. (1992). The essence of school renewal: The prose has begun. *Educational Leadership, 50,* 24–27.

Howey, K., and Vaughn, J. (1983). Current patterns of school improvement. In Griffin, G. A. (Ed.), *School improvement, eighty-second yearbook of the National Society for the Study of Education.* Chicago: University of Chicago Press, 92–117.

Johnston, S. (1990). Understanding curriculum decision-making through teacher images. *Journal of Curriculum Studies, 22,* 464.

Kirst, M. (1988). The internal allocation of resources within U.S. school districts: Implications for policy makers and practitioners. In D. H. Monk & J. Underwood (Eds.), *Micro level school finance* (pp. 365–389). Ninth Annual Yearbook of the American Finance Association. Cambridge, Mass.: Ballinger Publishing Company.

Latham, G., and Fifield, K. (1993). The hidden costs of teaching. *Educational Leadership, 50*(6), 44–45.

McHenry, C. D. (1989). Dedication versus professionalism. *Arkansas Educator, 14,* 2.

Moore, L. (1992). *Picking up the slack: Teachers subsidizing the system.* Unpublished Master's Degree Research Paper. Southern Illinois University, Carbondale.

Odden, A. R., and Picus, L. O. (1992). *School finance: A policy perspective.* New York: McGraw-Hill.

Wheeling, Illinois School District 21, (1987). Unpublished documents, newsletters, minutes, and reports of the School Improvement Committee.

Appendix

The following activities are intended to be used to review, practice, and implement literacy learning improvements in classrooms, schools, and districts. Depending upon the setting, these inquiry-based activities are useful as action-research assignments in classes, small-group activities in workshops, and collaborative efforts to improve the teaching of reading and writing in schools.

Activities 1 and 2 [Use with Chapters 1 and 2]

1. Use the sample or construct your own questionnaire and survey or interview your fellow teachers about reading/writing practices at your school. If you can, try to include the principal or parents. Summarize the results and prepare a concise report. Share the results and the report with others at school. What did you find out? Was there agreement? Do you perceive that changes in literacy learning might be possible? Are some teachers already making changes? What do you predict about future changes in reading/writing instruction at your school?

Here is a sample questionnaire that teachers developed as part of an inquiry-based school improvement plan. Notice that each item is rated by importance and extent of use. This two-level response format provides a way to help teachers decide which items are worthy of becoming literacy improvement targets. For example, an item rated high in importance and low in use indicates a possible area for improvement. On the other hand, an item rated low in importance and high in use indicates a practice that could possibly be discontinued.

Sample Questionnaire

Reading professionals suggest that the following eleven strategies are important in the development of strategic readers. Please share with us the extent to which you value as well as implement each individual strategy. Read each statement below and circle a rating for each of the two categories: importance and extent of use. Rate your answers using the following scales:

IMPORTANCE		
1 = Not Important	2 = Somewhat Important	3 = Very Important
EXTENT OF USE		
1 = Never	2 = Sometimes	3 = Regularly

Please return this survey to _____ by _____.

Thank you for your cooperation!!!

READING SURVEY

Grade Level(s) _____

	IMPORTANCE			EXTENT OF USE		
	Not	Somewhat	Very	Never	Sometimes	Regularly
1. I have students use their background knowledge to predict what they will read.	1	2	3	1	2	3
2. I help students learn about text structure to assist them in figuring out what is most important.	1	2	3	1	2	3
3. I have students work in groups to map whole texts or parts of texts.	1	2	3	1	2	3
4. I use several types of questions to guide discussion about selections students read.	1	2	3	1	2	3
5. I promote diverse thinking among students in responses to discussion questions.	1	2	3	1	2	3
6. I encourage students to share the cognitive strategies that they use to generate answers and overcome reading roadblocks.	1	2	3	1	2	3
7. I ask questions that require students to apply what they have read to other parts of their lives.	1	2	3	1	2	3

8. I have students work together to complete skill and/or strategy assignments.	1	2	3	1	2	3
9. I have students do activities that require them to evaluate rather than simply recall information.	1	2	3	1	2	3
10. Over time, I help students learn that they must vary their reading strategies to meet the demands of different texts, purposes, and expectations.	1	2	3	1	2	3
11. I encourage students to discuss and monitor their reading habits and attitudes.	1	2	3	1	2	3

2. Assume that several teachers have talked about approaching the rest of the teachers in their school about initiating a parent involvement program that will improve communication and gain more community support. Consider the change-agent behaviors discussed near the end of the chapter.

- Build credibility in school and community
- Participate in professional organizations
- Engage in personal lifelong learning
- Interact with mentors
- Write, reflect, tell your story
- Network with other teachers
- Seek funds to improve schools
- Be resilient
- Be proactive

Discuss these with other teachers. Write a short paper that responds to the following questions: Do these behaviors suggest any courses of action? Which of these behaviors are most relevant? Which are the least relevant? What risks are apparent for the teachers who want to initiate a parent involvement program? If these teachers approached you what would your reaction be?

Activities 3 and 4 [Use with Chapters 3 and 4]

3. Assume that a principal and the teachers are trying to decide when they might work together on a reading/writing improvement project. Use the following questionnaire. One of the barriers to changing teaching practices is related to the timing of school improvement activities. Teachers legitimately complain not only about a lack of time for making changes, they also complain about when improvement activities are scheduled. What is the best time for you to get the most value out of the reading and writing improvement activities?

Most Value				Least Value	
5	4	3	2	1	A. Saturday (8:30–11:30am)
5	4	3	2	1	B. After School (4–7pm)
5	4	3	2	1	C. Early Dismissal (1:30–4:30pm)
5	4	3	2	1	D. Half Day Release
5	4	3	2	1	E. Full Day Release
5	4	3	2	1	F. Before School
5	4	3	2	1	G. After School
5	4	3	2	1	H. Other _____

Comments/Questions/Suggestions

A good way to do this activity is to ask each teacher to write his or her top time preference on a slip of paper. These individual ballots are collected, tallied, and the results are posted. This final tally represents the combination of individual responses and collective balloting. The significant feature of this is that everyone participates by writing alone before anything is discussed.

4.   This is a team activity in content literacy that has been used successfully with upper elementary grade teachers. The goal is to have teachers collaborate on ways to improve students content literacy skills. The first step is to use a questionnaire with teachers and an interview with students (the same questions) about reading and learning from science, social studies, and mathematics texts.

Try to get responses from each teacher. If some do not respond, one reminder is a tactful way to get busy teachers to reply. In any case do not harass anyone who declines. Remember, the goal is to get teachers to volunteer. Do not interview all of the students. A good plan is to get a random sample of about 25 percent. The next step is to summarize and share the results with other teachers in a brief written report. Next, meet with interested volunteers (remember the refreshments) and discuss the results. At this meeting make sure that there is an equal focus on both strengths and concerns. The goal is to get at least two (hopefully more) teachers interested in learning some strategies for improving the content literacy skills of students.

Teacher Questionnaire

Please respond to the following questions about science, social studies, and mathematics texts you are currently using. Your personal response will remain confidential. Rate each item using the following scale:

1—Never	2—Seldom	3—Often	4—Always

	Science	Soc. Stds.	Math
1. I provide pre-reading activities before students read assignments in . . .	1 2 3 4	1 2 3 4	1 2 3 4
2. Students have ample time in class to read textbooks in . . .	1 2 3 4	1 2 3 4	1 2 3 4
3. Students are taught how to summarize the important points in . . .	1 2 3 4	1 2 3 4	1 2 3 4
4. Students are taught how to infer and construct meaning from texts in . . .	1 2 3 4	1 2 3 4	1 2 3 4
5. Students are taught how to read maps, graphs, tables, charts, in . . .	1 2 3 4	1 2 3 4	1 2 3 4
6. I provide study guides for students in . . .	1 2 3 4	1 2 3 4	1 2 3 4
7. I use cooperative learning groups to help students learn from texts in . . .	1 2 3 4	1 2 3 4	1 2 3 4
8. I teach new words and/or concepts before asking students to read texts in . . .	1 2 3 4	1 2 3 4	1 2 3 4
9. Students are taught how to determine word meanings from context in . . .	1 2 3 4	1 2 3 4	1 2 3 4
10. Additional help is provided students who are having difficulty reading in . . .	1 2 3 4	1 2 3 4	1 2 3 4

Student Interview

Suggestion: Ask the students their names and explain that their answers will be private. Teachers will be told how *most* people answered.

1. Is your science book easy or hard to read?

2. Is your social studies book easy or hard to read?

3. Are the directions, examples, story problems in your math book easy or hard to read?

4. Does your teacher help you with these books by telling you about new words, important ideas, or discussing what you will read *before* you read?

5. Do you have enough time in class to read your social studies book? Your science book?

Never   Seldom   Often   Always

6. Does your teacher show you how to read maps, graphs, tables, and charts that are in your texts?

Never   Seldom   Often   Always

7. Here is a paragraph [use a text the student uses] from one of your books. Read it and summarize what it is about in one or two sentences.

Can summarize well   Can summarize somewhat   Cannot summarize

8. Sometimes answers or important ideas are not stated directly in the text, but you know them and use them as you think about what you are reading. If they are not in the book where do they come from? For example, read the sentence "She asked for size seven in white." Who could she be? What is she asking for?

Inferred easily   Had some difficulty inferring   Did not infer responses

9. Does your teacher provide study guides to help you learn from your social studies, science, or math books?

10. Do you ever work in a small group and read the same material and answer the same questions together with other students?

Use the data from these two sources as a basis for a discussion. For example, in one school that did this there was high agreement between teachers and students regarding the following: Time—both said there was ample time to read assignments in class. Maps, graphs, tables—both said students were helped with these before they read. There was less agreement on these points: *Summarizing.* Teachers said they taught summarizing but the students said it was very hard to do. Over 60 percent of the students who were studied had difficulty summarizing the paragraph in one or two sentences. *Constructing meaning with inferences.* Both teachers and students agreed that this had not been dealt with very much. At a meeting over the lunch hour, seven teachers agreed to meet again to plan ways to help students write good summaries. In addition, the teachers agreed to explore ways to improve the inference strategies of students. Data collection by teachers is a way to begin dialogue, seek consensus, collaborate, and approach literacy improvement on a team basis.

The final result of this exercise will be a short list of concerns that teachers have constructed based on data from their own classrooms. A good way to seal their commitment to a collaborative effort is to have each teacher sign his or her name at the bottom of the list—creating a declaration of collaboration.

Activity 5 [Use with Chapter 5]

5. Review the eight dance steps presented in Chapter 5 and write an eight-paragraph description of how they would be followed when teachers replace the old practice of round-robin reading with more effective oral reading activities. In this exercise you will see that the first two steps (forming a team and setting priorities) are already completed. In addition, six alternatives for round-robin reading are also described below. They are provided as possible ideas you can consider. Of course, other oral reading alternatives can be selected in order to complete this activity. The goal of this is to try out and reflect how the eight-step procedure will help teachers move away from the current (round-robin reading) practice toward new and more effective oral reading practices.

Alternatives for Round-Robin Reading

Repeated reading: In repeated reading, students reread the same selection or part of a passage orally until they read the material quickly and smoothly. A longer passage can be divided into short, but meaningful, sections of 100 to 200 words. The goal is to have students fluently read the passage at about 80 to 100 words per minute with 98 to 100 percent word-recognition accuracy. Students can do this alone or with a partner. Often they will be able to master a passage and "perform" it with about six practices before moving on to another. At the initial stages, when the material is unfamiliar, a taped rendition (see below) can be used to assist students.

Teacher-assisted and/or tape-assisted reading: In this type of reading, the teacher reads with the students and when the students begin to recognize the words, the teacher pauses and lets the students read alone. They continue, with the teacher quickly filling in any words that are not recognized after one or two seconds. In tape-assisted reading, students look at the book, listen to a tape of the text, and read along with it until they are able to fluently read without the tape.

Partner reading: Students work in pairs, with one student designated the listener and the other the reader. By skimming the selection, the partners together designate a question to be answered from the reading. Students alternate, with one student reading a section and the other listening. After a student has finished a turn reading, the listener gives a response to the question. The reader verifies the response by referring back to the text.

Individuals read within a group: When students read a section of a passage aloud to a small group or the whole class there should be an apparent reason for reading and listening. One way to do this is to have students locate a sentence or section of a passage that confirmed a prediction. This activity calls for students to state their prediction and then read the confirming material. Other students are to listen, rather than following along in their books. While they are listening their role is to think if the prediction and the passage make sense. Their role is not to catch the reader at mispronouncing or misreading a word. This activity gives students a reason for reading aloud and for listening carefully.

Choral reading: Choral reading is characterized by having groups or even the whole class read aloud in unison. There are several variations or patterns to follow, such as a small group can alternate stanzas of a poem, or a large group can read a song refrain, while individuals or pairs read verses.

Readers' theater: In this activity a play is used and the script is read orally. Students do not memorize parts nor do they perform the scenes with movement and costumes. The intent is to promote oral reading fluency with materials that follow the story structure of a play. Students take roles and read their "lines" while others listen to the play. Roles can rotate and different groups can orally "perform" the same play. Again, the focus on this reading activity is to make oral reading as meaningful and interesting as possible.

Use the following guide to complete this activity. Each step is already listed for you. Read the hints, questions, and write responses for each step.

1. *An Improvement Team Is Formed.*
     Representative teachers from each grade level, the principal, and two parents have been meeting for two months. During this time they have agreed to try to follow an eight-step plan for changing some of the classroom reading/writing activities.

2. The Team Sets Priorities for Change.

Based upon grade level discussions, and especially the urging of three teachers and the principal, the team decided that a good place to begin was to try to replace round-robin oral reading with more meaningful and interesting activities. One reason for selecting this rather narrow topic was the fact that some teachers were already using other alternatives. Another was that because the eight-step procedure itself was a new "way of life" for the school, they wanted to try it out on a relatively clear and straightforward issue—classroom oral reading practices.

At this point in this activity you are to write your own plans following the rest of the eight steps.

3. Choose the Critical Dimensions for Change.

Recall the six dimensions of teaching and decide which ones will need to be altered, or left alone, when round-robin oral reading is replaced. In about one page or so draft a response that addresses the following question: Will implementing alternate oral reading practices alter the school reading and writing goals and objectives, content, teaching strategies, materials and resources, assessment procedures, or classroom management?

4. Develop a Description of Full Implementation.

Based upon the response to the previous step in the procedure, what will full implementation look like? Again, in about a page or so, describe what the ideal oral reading practices might be in a typical classroom. These will differ depending upon the grade levels, but try to "image" which oral reading practices will be most preferred in several given situations.

5. Describe the Current Status and Stages of Growth.

Again, in a page or so, describe the current use of round-robin oral reading as well as the current use of other alternatives. Then predict and make a time line of when alternatives will be introduced, tried out, talked about, and hopefully adopted. These time lines will reflect individual differences. Some teachers will be close to full implementation while others will be only starting. Consider if teachers want to observe each other, help each other, or go it alone. Here is where specific obstacles to growth will appear.

6. Assess Obstacles to Growth.

What will prevent teachers from changing? Listen carefully and do not ignore or dismiss this information. Make lists, discuss the problems, and try to select some action or activity to overcome each obstacle. For example, one obstacle to the use of reader's theater idea may be a lack of suitable plays/scripts and a lack of multiple copies. The obvious solution is to obtain quantities of suitable materials.

7. *Implement Change Strategies.*
   A. Develop task-name-time documents using the following format. Here is where you will select specific subtasks to overcome specific obstacles and move closer to the "ideal" practices you have previously described in step four.

Goal: Replace round-robin oral reading with more effective activities

Subtask	Person(s) Responsible	Date/Time
Purchase plays		

B. Write a memo similar to the example memo on page 12. Use the stages (Awareness/Interest; Mental Tryout and Trials; Adoption, Integration, Continuation) as a guide to the content of your memo to the staff.

8. *Monitor Progress.*
   Set dates for meeting where teachers can report progress, discuss problems, and share successes. Decide on how to assess teacher and student attitudes toward the new practices. Be prepared to deal with new concerns, to adjust time lines, and to be ready to go back to step three to remember your original objective.

Activity 6 [Use with Chapter 6]

6.   Use the participatory ranking format described in Chapter 6 and the sample teacher questions that are listed below. Have a faculty or group of teachers prioritize their major concerns about a teaching topic. I have used this with good results on the broad topic of working and learning conditions as well as narrower issues related to literacy. For example, a broad approach would be to ask a group of teachers to list three ideas they have about improving the working conditions for themselves and the learning conditions for students. A narrower approach would be to ask teachers to list reasons why students don't reach their full reading and writing potential. Another would be to ask teachers to list three attributes of a strategic reader. Whatever you ask will control the listings the teachers make. This prioritized list has the potential to become a list of concerns, goals, or shared agreements that lead teachers to work together on common school improvement goals.

Sample Teacher Questions

- List at least three ideas that you have for improving the working conditions for teachers and the learning conditions for students at this school.
- What prevents students from reaching their full reading and writing potential?
- What are at least three attributes of a strategic reader?

Activities 7, 8, 9, and 10 [Use with Chapters 7, 8, 9]

7. Write a minimanual for your classroom following the steps described in Chapter 7. Share it with another teacher. Share it with the principal. What did you learn as you wrote it? What problems did you encounter trying to write your own manual? What did you learn when you shared it with the teacher? What did the principal say? Would this work for your entire grade level or the school?

8. Plan a classroom or school activity that involves parents and/or the community in a literacy celebration. Use some of the ideas in Chapter 8 or come up with your own idea. Try to keep it simple and successful so that a positive celebration might be repeated or expanded in the future. The celebration may involve parents or others from the community speaking in your room or school. Try to show how reading and writing are important to specific jobs, services, and hobbies to adults from different settings in your community.

9. Examine the five guidelines presented in Chapter 9 that tell how schools are changing the financial policies that relate to school improvement. Write a brief account of how you would present these ideas to the administration, the school board, the teachers' union as ways to better support grass-roots school improvement.

10. Use the grant format and the guidelines for developing and submitting grants that are described in Chapter 9. Develop a proposal and write a narrative describing one or more sections. Share your outline and sections you have written with other teachers, the principal, or other school officials. What is their reaction? Are you motivated to keep going?

Index